Praise for
A Month with *Messiah*

Gary Holloway's passion to link meditations with *Messiah* is a great ministry. Handel's work is a microcosm of the entirety of human existence, from the Fall to the Final Redemption. It provides fertile ground for offering views of solutions to the myriad temptations we face on a daily basis.

—**Gregory S. Athnos,** author of *Handel's Messiah: A New View of Its Musical and Spiritual Architecture*

A MONTH WITH MESSIAH

31 BIBLICAL MEDITATIONS ON HANDEL'S MASTERWORK

BY

GARY HOLLOWAY

Published by KHARIS PUBLISHING, an imprint of KHARIS MEDIA LLC.

Copyright © 2025 Gary Holloway

ISBN-13: 978-1-63746-374-1

ISBN-10: 1-63746-374-X

Library of Congress Control Number: 2025945670

All KHARIS PUBLISHING products are available at special quantity discounts for bulk purchases for sales promotions, premiums, fund-raising, and educational needs. For details, contact:

Kharis Media LLC
Tel: 1-630-909-3405
support@kharispublishing.com
www.kharispublishing.com

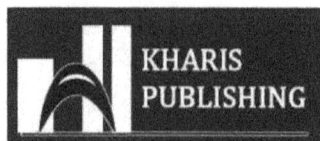

Contents

INTRODUCTION

What a thrill to hear *Messiah* by George Frideric Handel (1685-1759)! Although its premier performance was at Easter 1742, in a secular setting in Dublin, Ireland, we associate it with the Christmas season. Yet on any given day, somewhere in the world, a choir is singing *Messiah*. The matchless composition is 283 years old this year. Ludwig van Beethoven said Handel was "the greatest composer who ever lived." Certainly, today we have GOATs…Greatest of All Times in this or that sport or endeavor, but to have one "greatest composer of all time," identify another composer as "the greatest of all time" is superlative praise, indeed.

The stunning beauty of Handel's score, completed in only twenty-four days in 1741, might blind us to the power of the texts chosen by Charles Jennens (1700-1773). Adapting from the King James Version of the Bible (1611) and The Book of Common Prayer (1549), Jennens uses the Scriptures to tell the story of Jesus as the Messiah from before His birth through His death and resurrection to His glorification.

Next to the Bible, nothing shapes our faith more than the hymns we sing. The majesty of the music of *Messiah* enhances the power of these words from Scripture. As we let those words sink deeply into our hearts, the Holy Spirit will lead us into a deeper experience of the Jesus, the Messiah, we long to see.

HOW TO USE THIS DEVOTIONAL GUIDE

This devotional guide is based on two firm convictions: First, that God is at work within us and among us. Second, that we are not the first God has worked within and among. Each daily devotional here brings you in touch with the faith of those who for nearly three centuries have experienced God through singing and hearing these words.

Each day begins with a portion from the Bible verses in *Messiah*, giving a direction for the day, a signpost of how God is working in us. This allows us to hear God's voice in His word, the Bible, and to let God shape our day and our lives. It would be good to listen to a recording of those words in *Messiah*, or to sing those words from memory. Then read those verses slowly. Meditate on them. To help, there is an extended reflection on those verses in their original biblical context. At the end of the reflection there are questions to lead you deeper into the mystery of God's gift of Jesus as the Messiah. After that, there are suggestions on how to live out the call to follow the Messiah. These are meant to be gracious ideas for our "to be" and "to do" list for the day. A brief prayer thought ends each devotional.

Thus this book can lead you into a time alone with God each day. This can be a devotion lasting a few minutes or you can extend it by singing again the section from *Messiah* and by examining the Scripture passages in their wider context. The short prayer can also act as a prayer starter that leads you into a longer and deeper period of prayer.

This approach can also shape family worship or small group study. If each member of the family or group has already reflected on that day's devotion, then each can share the word they heard from God that day. This will lead into a time of group meditation.

A WORD OF ENCOURAGEMENT
Our Messiah, Jesus, desires to spend time with us. As we take a few minutes each day to listen to the music of His great love, expressed in these words from the Bible, Jesus Himself will be with us through His Holy Spirit. Spending time with the Messiah takes consistent discipline; at first, what may be a thrill soon turns into a daily task. In sticking to our pledge to be alone with God each day, particularly when we are busy or we don't feel like it, we receive a greater blessing.

We learn, no matter what the day brings, to sing with our lives, "Hallelujah, for the Lord God omnipotent reigneth!"

DAY ONE:
COMFORT

"Comfort ye, comfort ye my people, saith your God. Speak ye comfortably to Jerusalem, and cry unto her, that her warfare is accomplished, that her iniquity is pardoned." *Isaiah 40:1*

Comfort.

I like comfort. I sleep on a comfortable pillow in a comfortable bed. I awake to a house that is warm in the winter and cool in the summer. If you could see me, you would know that I prefer comfort to fashion in my clothing. Financially, I am not rich, but I am comfortably well-off. Even in my relationships, I prefer being with my comfortable old friends to meeting strangers.

I may be addicted to comfort. I don't think I am alone. We Americans spend much of our money, time, and effort trying to be a bit more comfortable. What's wrong with that? Shouldn't we be even more comfortable?

The Danger of Being Comfortable

God never promised His people they would be comfortable. He even warns them of the dangers of comfort. When Israel is about to enter the Promised Land with all its comforts, they receive this caution:

> "But that is the time to be careful! Beware that in your plenty you do not forget the Lord your God and disobey his commands, regulations, and decrees that I am giving you today. For when you have become full and prosperous and have built fine homes to live in, and when your flocks and herds have become very large and your silver and gold have multiplied along with everything else, be careful! Do not become proud at that time and forget the Lord your God, who rescued you from slavery in the land of Egypt. Do not forget that he led you through the great and terrifying wilderness with its poisonous snakes and scorpions, where it was so hot and dry. He gave you water from the rock! He fed you with manna in the wilderness, a food unknown to your ancestors. He did this to humble you and test you for your own good. He did all this so you would never say to yourself, 'I have achieved this wealth with my own strength and energy.'" *Deuteronomy 8:11-17*

It is not wrong to be comfortable, but it is dangerous. We may forget that the Lord is the only source of our comfort and prosperity. Comfort easily becomes an idol.

The Discomforting Call

Jesus calls His followers not to comfort, but to suffering and death.

> Then he said to the crowd, "If any of you wants to be my follower, you must give up your own way, take up your cross daily, and follow me. If you try to hang on to your

life, you will lose it. But if you give up your life for my sake, you will save it." *Luke 9:23-24*

God does not promise that His people will be comfortable. The good news is that He does promise to comfort them. This comfort is not taking it easy, but is the help God gives us when we are most desperate and at the end of our rope.

Comfort to Israel

Messiah begins with this word of comfort from Isaiah. Why did God's people need comfort in Isaiah's day? Because in spite of the warnings from God's prophet, Israel had turned away from the Lord. Because of that rebellion, God had sent them into exile. Exile is the opposite of comfort. God's people might be tempted to despair, thinking that the Lord would never forgive them, but the discomfort of exile leads them to call upon the Lord in their desperation.

And the Lord answers! He promises to comfort His people. This is the theme of the last part of Isaiah. God comforts by acting to relieve their suffering (Isaiah 49:13), to give them joy (Isaiah 51:3), to take away their fear (Isaiah 51:12), to redeem them (Isaiah 52:9), to heal them (Isaiah 57:18), to mend their broken hearts (Isaiah 61:1), and to be like a mother to them (Isaiah 66:13). Each of these verses uses the word "comfort" to speak of the restoring work of the Lord.

Comforted to Comfort

Jesus embodies the comfort promised in Isaiah. He teaches, heals, redeems, and restores us. Yes, He shakes us out of our comfort zone, calling us to suffer and die with Him, and He promises that if we give up our lives we will save them.

Our comfortable lifestyles may keep us from being hopeless enough to put our hope in Him. He promises comfort to those who mourn (Matthew 5:4). He heals those whose cases are beyond the help of physicians (Mark 5:24-29). It is hard to sincerely pray for daily bread when our refrigerators are full of food. Like Israel, we need to experience exile more deeply to turn our hearts to the only one who can comfort us. So if you feel hopeless, unable to find comfort from anyone or anything, there is good news. God promises His comfort in Jesus.

> **Praise be to the God and Father of our Lord Jesus Christ, the Father of compassion and the God of all comfort, who comforts us in all our troubles, so that we can comfort those in any trouble with the comfort we ourselves receive from God. For just as we share abundantly in the sufferings of Christ, so also our comfort abounds through Christ. If we are distressed, it is for your comfort and salvation; if we are comforted, it is for your comfort, which produces in you patient endurance of the same sufferings we suffer. And our hope for you is firm, because we know that just as you share in our sufferings, so also you share in our comfort.**
> *2 Corinthians 1:3-7 (NIV)*

Paul tells the Corinthians that God has comforted them through Christ so they in turn can comfort others. Which brings us back to Isaiah chapter 40. Who is addressed when the Lord says, "Comfort ye my people?" Who is the "ye" (or y'all or you guys) who is to comfort Israel? It is ultimately God who provides that comfort, but He calls on others—perhaps the prophets—to announce that word of comfort.

In the same way, we Christians are to bring a word of comfort to our world. To our shame, many hear only words of condemnation from us. Yes, like Isaiah and the prophets, we must sometimes announce God's words of warning and judgment, but those are never the last words. God comforts His creation by giving His Son not to judge the world but to save it (John 3:16-17). Peace and pardon are the comforting words that begin *Messiah*. That is the good news we share with all those we meet.

For Reflection

1. How important is being comfortable to you? Is it too important?

2. Why would Jesus want us to be uncomfortable?

3. How does God comfort his people?

Living the Messiah

1. Fast or abstain from something you find comfortable today in order to help you rely more on Jesus.

2. Bring words of comfort to someone today.

Prayer

God of all comfort, renew us this day so we might comfort others with the Good News of Jesus.

DAY TWO:
HIGHWAY

The voice of him that crieth in the wilderness, "Prepare ye the way of the Lord, make straight in the desert a highway for our God."
Every valley shall be exalted, and every mountain and hill made low, the crooked straight, and the rough places plain. And the glory of the Lord shall be revealed, and all flesh shall see it together, for the mouth of the Lord hath spoken it. *Isaiah 40:3-5*

I live in a state where we do not want our taxes increased. As a result, we have terrible roads. Driving even on major highways means constantly weaving to avoid the potholes. Small and winding country roads are even worse. We do not need a sign to welcome us to a neighboring state. The lack of constant road noise and a bumpy ride let us know that we have made it to the land of road repair. I think I'd even pay more tax if I were sure our roads would be fixed.

Rough Road

My driving experience does not compare with what God's people faced after the Exodus from Egypt. God led them directly to the Promised Land, but when they got there, they did not trust the Lord enough to go in. So God made that unfaithful generation wander in the wilderness for forty years (Numbers 32:8-13).

Forty years! On long road trips I have often wondered if I would ever arrive. "Are we there yet?" is a question we frequently ask. To spend day after hot day travelling aimlessly in the desert for an entire generation is beyond my imagination.

God is faithful; He leads the next generation into the Promised Land. His power gives them victory over their enemies and they conquer the land. Yet even then, God's people often rebel against Him, serving other gods alongside the Lord. Eventually, in Isaiah's day, God sends them into exile.

Smooth Road

God is faithful and He promises they will return to the land if they turn to Him. Yet they had to ask themselves how easy that return might be. Would they have to roam for another forty years in this second Exodus?

Isaiah has great news! They will travel back through the desert on a super-highway. The Lord will level the mountains, raise the valleys, and make their way smooth, but who will travel on this highway?

It is not just a road for God's people. It is a road for the Lord himself. He will go before His people and lead them back to the land. After the first Exodus, God's people abandon Him at Sinai, worshipping a golden calf. The Lord then tells Moses that He will send an angel to lead the people to the land, but that God himself will not go with them.

"Go up to this land that flows with milk and honey. But I will not travel among you, for you are a stubborn and rebellious people. If I did, I would surely destroy you along the way."
Then Moses said, "If you don't personally go with us, don't make us leave this place. How will anyone know that you look favorably on me—on me and on your people—if you don't go with us? For your presence among us sets your people and me apart from all other people on the earth."
The Lord replied to Moses, "I will indeed do what you have asked, for I look favorably on you, and I know you by name." *Exodus 33:3, 15-17*

The Lord relents and agrees to go with them. Isaiah says that in this second Exodus from exile, God will lead them on a straight and smooth path.

A Road for All

This gentle, trouble-free road is not just for Israel but for everyone. "All flesh" will see the glory of the Lord. These words from Isaiah point to an ultimate Exodus experience for all people. God will free them from their slavery to sin and reveal His glory to them.

Jesus leads all people from bondage to sin to the final Promised Land. That's why all four Gospels use these words of Isaiah to describe the work of John the Baptist (Matthew 3:1-3, Mark 1:1-8, Luke 3:3-6, John 1:19-27). The Gospel of Mark begins with these words:

The beginning of the good news about Jesus the Messiah, the Son of God, as it is written in Isaiah the prophet:
"I will send my messenger ahead of you,
who will prepare your way"—
"a voice of one calling in the wilderness,

> 'Prepare the way for the Lord,
>   make straight paths for him.'"
>
> And so John the Baptist appeared in the wilderness, preaching a baptism of repentance for the forgiveness of sins. The whole Judean countryside and all the people of Jerusalem went out to him. Confessing their sins, they were baptized by him in the Jordan River. John wore clothing made of camel's hair, with a leather belt around his waist, and he ate locusts and wild honey. And this was his message: "After me comes the one more powerful than I, the straps of whose sandals I am not worthy to stoop down and untie. I baptize you with water, but he will baptize you with the Holy Spirit." *Mark 1:1-8 (NIV)*

John comes to the wilderness to introduce one who will lead us out of the wilderness. He points to one who is God made flesh, displaying the glory of God.

> So the Word became human and made his home among us. He was full of unfailing love and faithfulness. And we have seen his glory, the glory of the Father's one and only Son. *John 1:14*

What was good news in Isaiah's day is even better news for us. Like the Diana Ross song (written by Nickolas Ashford and Valerie Simpson, 1966), there "…ain't no mountain high enough, ain't no valley low enough, ain't no river wide enough" to keep God from getting to His people. God takes the highway from heaven to become human in Jesus. Jesus humbles Himself to die for us, leading us on the highway to heaven, the ultimate Promised Land. He ascends to the Father and will come again so all will see the glory of God.

Therefore, God elevated him to the place of highest honor
and gave him the name above all other names,
that at the name of Jesus every knee should bow,
in heaven and on earth and under the earth,
and every tongue declare that Jesus Christ is Lord,
to the glory of God the Father. *Philippians 2:9-11*

For Reflection

1. Why did the Lord make Israel wander in the wilderness for forty years? How was this an act of love?

2. How does John the Baptist act like the voice in the wilderness in Isaiah?

3. How is the coming of Jesus the Messiah like a new Exodus?

Living the Messiah

1. With the heart of Jesus, do what you can to make someone's path easy this day.

2. Take time to meditate on what the mouth of the Lord has spoken in these verses.

Prayer

Loving God, nothing can keep you from coming to us. May we make a highway into our lives for you to enter us today. Lord Jesus, we give God the glory for all you have done for us.

DAY THREE:
SHAKING

Thus saith the Lord of Hosts; yet once, a little while, and I will shake the heavens, and the earth, the sea, and the dry land; And I will shake all nations; and the Desire of All Nations shall come. *Haggai 2:6-7*

Several years ago I woke in the middle of the night with my bed shaking. It was a mild earthquake, so mild that my wife did not even wake up. It was still a frightening experience, but my fear pales in comparison to those who have been through life-threatening earthquakes.

Earthquakes, physical and metaphorical, remind us that we cannot even depend on the ground beneath our feet.

Shake Down

Haggai tells the story of a small group of exiles who have returned to Judah after the exile. They build fine houses for themselves but neglect to rebuild the temple. Haggai the prophet, Zerubbabel the prefect, and Jehozadak the high priest encouraged them to build the house of the Lord (Haggai 1:1-15). Those who remember the splendor of

Solomon's temple know that they do not have the resources to reconstruct the temple in the fullness of its glory (Haggai 2:1-3).

The Lord promises that he will provide what is needed for building the temple. He will shake the nations so their wealth will flow to Judah. This shakedown is not robbing the nations because all belongs to the Lord.

> **"The silver is mine, and the gold is mine, says the Lord of Heaven's Armies. The future glory of this Temple will be greater than its past glory, says the Lord of Heaven's Armies. And in this place I will bring peace. I, the Lord of Heaven's Armies, have spoken!"** *Haggai 2:8-9*

The Lord in the Earthquake

This is not the only time the Bible describes the powerful work of God as an earthquake. When the Lord descends on Sinai to give his people his instruction,

> **All of Mount Sinai was covered with smoke because the Lord had descended on it in the form of fire. The smoke billowed into the sky like smoke from a brick kiln, and the whole mountain shook violently.** *Exodus 19:18*

The glory of God was so present that the earth could not contain it without shaking. Often in the Bible, when the Lord appears, He shakes the earth (Judges 5:4, Psalm 68:8, Isaiah 6:4, Habakkuk 3:6). Sometimes that shaking represents the anger of God against rebellion (Numbers 16:31-34, 2 Samuel 22:8; Psalm 18:7, Nahum 1:5, Revelation 6:12-17, 11:3, 16:17-21). At other times, it is the Lord who protects his people when the earth quakes (Psalm 46:1-2).

God is in control of His world. When His people begin to think they are in control, when they are comfortable in their prosperity, He shakes things up. When God's people think they are too small to do the work God has given them, He shakes blessings loose so they can do His will. God shakes His creation in order to bless it.

Shaking and the Desire of All Nations

In Haggai, the "Desire of All Nations" is the wealth that God will shake loose for the rebuilding of the temple. The ultimate desire of all nations is for the Messiah to come and bless the world. Christians understand the Desire of All Nations refers to Jesus (that's why the term is capitalized in the lyrics of *Messiah*).

So we are not surprised that shaking and earthquakes accompany the death and resurrection of Jesus.

> **And when Jesus had cried out again in a loud voice, he gave up his spirit.**
> **At that moment the curtain of the temple was torn in two from top to bottom. The earth shook, the rocks split and the tombs broke open. The bodies of many holy people who had died were raised to life. They came out of the tombs after Jesus' resurrection and went into the holy city and appeared to many people.**
> **When the centurion and those with him who were guarding Jesus saw the earthquake and all that had happened, they were terrified, and exclaimed, "Surely he was the Son of God!"** *Matthew 27:50-54 (NIV)*

Perhaps this earthquake showed the judgment of God against those who put Jesus to death. However, the resurrection of the godly here in Matthew prefigures final resurrection of the saints where God shakes away the old order to inaugurate a new heaven and earth.

> **After the Sabbath, at dawn on the first day of the week, Mary Magdalene and the other Mary went to look at the tomb.**
> **There was a violent earthquake, for an angel of the Lord came down from heaven and, going to the tomb, rolled**

back the stone and sat on it. His appearance was like lightning, and his clothes were white as snow. The guards were so afraid of him that they shook and became like dead men.

The angel said to the women, "Do not be afraid, for I know that you are looking for Jesus, who was crucified. He is not here; he has risen, just as he said. Come and see the place where he lay. Then go quickly and tell his disciples: 'He has risen from the dead and is going ahead of you into Galilee. There you will see him.' Now I have told you." *Matthew 28:1-7 (NIV)*

The earthquake of the death and resurrection of Jesus has altered the landscape of our world. God has shaken the nations so the greatest riches of all—salvation through Our Messiah—will flow, not out of, but into every nation.

The Unshakable Kingdom

All this talk of shaking and earthquakes makes us long for a place where we can stand secure. The Book of Hebrews uses the passage where God shakes the earth to speak of a solid assurance of the new heaven and earth.

When God spoke from Mount Sinai his voice shook the earth, but now he makes another promise: "Once again I will shake not only the earth but the heavens also." This means that all of creation will be shaken and removed, so that only unshakable things will remain.
Since we are receiving a Kingdom that is unshakable, let us be thankful and please God by worshiping him with holy fear and awe. *Hebrews 12:26-28*

The Lord shakes the earth at Sinai. He shakes kingdoms in His judgment. He restructures all creation in the death and resurrection of Jesus. He pours all riches into His people, His temple, through the

24

Desire of All Nations. Charles Wesley, in *Hark the Herald Angels Sing*, uses this phrase to praise God for the incarnation, "Come, Desire of Nations, come, fix in us thy humble home."

So we give thanks to the God who shakes the heavens and the earth in order to give us a kingdom that cannot be shaken, the kingdom of the Messiah.

For Reflection

1. Why was there an earthquake at the death and resurrection of Jesus?

2. Fear is the usual reaction to an earthquake. Should we be afraid of God?

3. What might it take for God to shake you out of your comfortable indifference?

Living the Messiah

1. Think back on an event that rocked your world and shook your faith. What was God doing in that event?

2. Help someone whose life has been jolted by a tragedy.

Prayer

Frightening God, shake lose the blessings we need this day. Shake us out of our apathy. May we trust you to protect us from every earthquake in our lives. Make our trust in you unshakable.

DAY FOUR:
TEMPLE

The Lord, whom ye seek, shall suddenly come to His temple, even the messenger of the covenant, whom you delight in: behold, He shall come, saith the Lord of hosts.
But who may abide the day of His coming? and who shall stand when He appeareth? For He is like a refiner's fire.
And He shall purify the sons of Levi, that they may offer unto the Lord an offering in righteousness.
Malachi 3:1-3

I have been blessed to visit some of the most beautiful churches and cathedrals in the world. As one enters, the eyes are drawn heavenward, toward the soaring ceiling. The story of the Bible surrounds one in stained glass, mosaics, and frescos. The saints, apostles, and martyrs tell their stories through beautiful art. The one who gave Himself on the cross is the central focus. When you remember that believers spent decades, even centuries, shaping and building these offerings to their Lord, you cannot help but think, "God is present here."

The Lord in His Temple

Those who came to the temple in Jerusalem felt an even deeper sense of the presence of God. The building itself was majestic and beautiful, but what made it unique was that the Lord of the Universe promised to meet His people there. When Solomon dedicates the temple, his prayer makes it clear that no building can contain the Almighty, but he asks that the Lord will hear prayers made there.

> **"But will God really dwell on earth? The heavens, even the highest heaven, cannot contain you. How much less this temple I have built! Yet give attention to your servant's prayer and his plea for mercy, Lord my God. Hear the cry and the prayer that your servant is praying in your presence this day. May your eyes be open toward this temple night and day, this place of which you said, 'My Name shall be there,' so that you will hear the prayer your servant prays toward this place. Hear the supplication of your servant and of your people Israel when they pray toward this place. Hear from heaven, your dwelling place, and when you hear, forgive."** *I Kings 8:27-30 (NIV)*

God places His Name on the temple and His glory fills it. That is why the loss of the temple during the exile was so devastating to God's people. Ezekiel even has a vision of the glory of the Lord departing from the temple (Ezekiel 10:18). In exile, God's people wondered if the Lord had abandoned them forever since they had abandoned Him.

That's why these words from Malachi are such good news. The Lord returns to His temple after the exile. He purifies those who make offerings to Him so they may again lead His people in righteousness. God is faithful and will hear again their prayers at His temple.

The Lord is the Temple

Jesus is the ultimate presence of God, the Word made flesh. As such, He also comes to the temple. At eight days old, His parents have Him circumcised and bring Him to the temple for purification. There two prophets—Simeon and Anna—praise God for the coming of the Messiah (Luke 2:21-38). At twelve years old, Mary and Joseph bring Him to the temple for Passover. After they leave Jerusalem, they cannot find Jesus. Frantic, they search for Him for three days, finally finding Hm in the temple. Jesus is surprised that they did not know where He would be.

> **"But why did you need to search?" he asked. "Didn't you know that I must be in my Father's house?" But they didn't understand what he meant.** *Luke 2:49-50*

Jesus comes to the temple in His ministry. On one occasion, the one who was purified in the temple as an infant now purifies the temple.

> **When they arrived back in Jerusalem, Jesus entered the Temple and began to drive out the people buying and selling animals for sacrifices. He knocked over the tables of the money changers and the chairs of those selling doves, and he stopped everyone from using the Temple as a marketplace. He said to them, "The Scriptures declare, 'My Temple will be called a house of prayer for all nations,' but you have turned it into a den of thieves."** *Mark 11:15-17*

Jesus claims the temple as His own, restoring it to its original purpose as a place of prayer. Jesus does more than go to the temple; He claims to be the temple.

> **"All right," Jesus replied. "Destroy this temple, and in three days I will raise it up."**
> **"What!" they exclaimed. "It has taken forty-six years to build this Temple, and you can rebuild it in three days?"**

But when Jesus said "this temple," he meant his own body. After he was raised from the dead, his disciples remembered he had said this, and they believed both the Scriptures and what Jesus had said. *John 2:19-22*

What did Jesus mean when he said his body was the temple? The temple was the place where priests offered sacrifices. Jesus is the preeminent priest and the final sacrifice (Hebrews 10:12). The temple is where God heard and answered prayer. Jesus is our intercessor in prayer (Hebrews 7:25). The glory of the Lord filled the temple. Jesus embodies God's glory in its fullness (John 1:14).

Priests and Temple

So Jesus is the Lord who comes to His temple. There He purifies the Levites to make sacrifices. Now, through Jesus as our temple, all who believe in Him are priests.

And you are living stones that God is building into his spiritual temple. What's more, you are his holy priests. Through the mediation of Jesus Christ, you offer spiritual sacrifices that please God. *1 Peter 2:5*

As priests, we intercede for others. We offer the sacrifices of praise and service (Hebrews 13:15-16). To be righteous priests, the Lord must purify us with His fire. This is not the fire of punishment, but the fire of God's refining love.

I will bring that group through the fire and make them pure.
I will refine them like silver and purify them like gold.
They will call on my name, and I will answer them.
I will say, 'These are my people,' and they will say, 'The Lord is our God.'" *Zechariah 13:9 (see also Psalm 66:10, Isaiah 1:25, 48:10)*

As the body of Christ, the church reconciles the world to God. Our lives are not without trouble, but God uses even the hard times to shape us into the precious temple and priests who praise God and serve others.

> These trials will show that your faith is genuine. It is being tested as fire tests and purifies gold—though your faith is far more precious than mere gold. So when your faith remains strong through many trials, it will bring you much praise and glory and honor on the day when Jesus Christ is revealed to the whole world. *1 Peter 1:7*

For Reflection

1. How are churches and cathedrals like the temple in Jerusalem? How are they different?

2. What were the purposes of the temple in Jerusalem?

3. God is everywhere. Are there particular places where the presence of God is stronger? Where?

Living the Messiah

1. Serve someone as a priest today.

2. Identify something in your life that the Lord needs to burn away in order to purify you as a priest. Offer that to God in prayer.

Prayer

Jesus, our High Priest and Temple, purify us so we might offer the sacrifices of praise and service. Through your Holy Spirit, live in us as your temples this day.

DAY FIVE:
IMMANUEL

Behold, a virgin shall conceive, and bear a son, and shall call His name Immanuel. "God with us."
Isaiah 7:14; Matthew 1:23

O thou that tellest good tidings to Zion, get thee up into the high mountain. O thou that tellest good tidings to Jerusalem, lift up thy voice with strength: lift it up, be not afraid: say unto the cities of Judah, Behold your God!
Isaiah 40:9

Did a virgin give birth in the time of Isaiah? Was Mary just a young woman and not a virgin when she gave birth to Jesus?

These questions betray a misunderstanding of the nature of biblical prophecy. Some think the words of the prophets pointed only to the far future of the time of Jesus. They had no immediate relevance to the prophet's time. Others say that the gospel writers misused the writings of the prophets, stretching their meaning to apply the words to Jesus. However, biblical prophecies many times have two meanings—a near meaning for the prophet's time and a far meaning for the time of the Messiah. When we read their words, we need interpretive bifocals to see both the near and the far meanings.

A Young Woman

So, these verses have a meaning for Isaiah's time. Judah faces destruction from the kings of Israel and Syria. God reassures Ahaz, the king of Judah, that He will protect Judah. The Lord even gives Ahaz a sign of this deliverance.

> **Again the Lord spoke to Ahaz, saying, "Ask a sign of the Lord your God; let it be deep as Sheol or high as heaven." But Ahaz said, "I will not ask, and I will not put the Lord to the test." Then Isaiah said, "Hear then, O house of David! Is it too little for you to weary mortals that you weary my God also? Therefore the Lord himself will give you a sign. Look, the young woman is with child and shall bear a son and shall name him Immanuel. He shall eat curds and honey by the time he knows how to refuse the evil and choose the good. For before the child knows how to refuse the evil and choose the good, the land before whose two kings you are in dread will be deserted." *Isaiah 7:10-16 (NRSV)***

Ahaz refuses to ask God for a sign. Why? He knows his Bible, "Do not put the Lord to the test" (Deuteronomy 6:16). These are the same words Jesus uses, when tempted by Satan (Matthew 4:7). Yet in this case, it is the Lord Himself who tells Ahaz to seek a sign. So the Lord gives a sign. What is that sign? It is not that a virgin will give birth in the time of Ahaz. Yes, many Bible versions translate the Hebrew word here "virgin" even though it means "young woman." They do this because they do not understand the near and the far prophetic vision.

The sign to Ahaz is not that a young woman would have a child. That would be an ordinary event. The sign is that while the child is still too young to distinguish good from evil, God will destroy the two kings who threaten Ahaz. The name of the child is significant, Immanuel, which means "God is with us." This is great news for Isaiah's day. The Lord has not abandoned His people in spite of their sins. He is still with them.

A Virgin

Years later when the gospel writers tell the story of the birth of Jesus, they remember this verse from Isaiah and see its deeper meaning.

> **Now the birth of Jesus Christ took place in this way. When his mother Mary had been betrothed to Joseph, before they came together she was found to be with child from the Holy Spirit. And her husband Joseph, being a just man and unwilling to put her to shame, resolved to divorce her quietly. But as he considered these things, behold, an angel of the Lord appeared to him in a dream, saying, "Joseph, son of David, do not fear to take Mary as your wife, for that which is conceived in her is from the Holy Spirit. She will bear a son, and you shall call his name Jesus, for he will save his people from their sins." All this took place to fulfill what the Lord had spoken by the prophet: "Behold, the virgin shall conceive and bear a son, and they shall call his name Immanuel" (which means, God with us). When Joseph woke from sleep, he did as the angel of the Lord commanded him: he took his wife, but knew her not until she had given birth to a son. And he called his name Jesus.** *Matthew 1:18-25 (ESV)*

Joseph receives his own sign, an angel in a dream who gives the far-sighted meaning of Isaiah 7. Mary is a virgin and the child in her is from the Holy Spirit. The child to be born from this virginal conception is the ultimate sign of God's presence. This child named

Immanuel does not only signify that God is with us, but that He is God made flesh, "God with us."

That understanding of Immanuel is supported by the verse from Isaiah 40. That verse follows the previous lines in *Messiah* about comfort and the voice crying in the wilderness, preparing the way for the Lord. In Isaiah, the Lord comes to reward and care for His people. When Mary gives birth to Jesus the Messiah, those who see Him can more fully say, "Behold your God!"

Jumping ahead in the story, Thomas sees Jesus after the resurrection and confesses Him as "My Lord and my God!" (John 20:28). Other Bible passages identify Jesus as God.

> **In the beginning the Word already existed. The Word was with God, and the Word was God.** *John 1:1*

> **For in Christ lives all the fullness of God in a human body.** *Colossians 2:9*

> **We should live in this evil world with wisdom, righteousness, and devotion to God, while we look forward with hope to that wonderful day when the glory of our great God and Savior, Jesus Christ, will be revealed.** *Titus 2:12-13*

> **But to the Son he says, "Your throne, O God, endures forever and ever. You rule with a scepter of justice."** *Hebrews 1:8*

These verses display the conviction of the early church that Jesus of Nazareth was God in the flesh. Christians do not believe that He gradually grew into being God. We confess that the baby born to the Virgin Mary was God from the beginning. What glad tidings to Zion and to the world! Behold, your God!

For Reflection

1. Can biblical prophecy have a meaning for when it was given and a somewhat different meaning for later? How does that work?

2. Should we ask the Lord for signs? Why does God give signs? What is the relationship between faith and signs?

3. Why is it important that Mary was a virgin when she gave birth to Jesus?

Living the Messiah

1. Set aside time to meditate on the meanings of Immanuel—"God is with us" and "God with us." Live today with the assurance of His presence in Jesus.

2. Share the good tidings that God has come to us by giving a small act of kindness or a gentle word to someone.

Prayer

God, our Father, thank you for becoming one of us through the birth of Jesus to the Virgin Mary. May we always know you are with us. May we tell that good news to others.

DAY SIX:
LIGHT

Arise, shine, for thy light is come, and the glory of the Lord is risen upon thee. *Isaiah 60:1*

The people that walked in darkness have seen a great light, and they that dwell in
the land of the shadow of death, upon them hath the light shined. *Isaiah 9:2*

When I was a child I wanted a nightlight in my room because I was afraid of the dark. I am no longer afraid of the dark in that way, but when I awake in the middle of the night and stumble blindly out of bed, I am grateful to still have a nightlight.

Light in the Darkness

Like many of the prophets, Isaiah has a strong word of judgment against God's people. They will know the darkness of defeat and exile. The good news is that darkness will not last.

> **Nevertheless, that time of darkness and despair will not go on forever. The land of Zebulun and Naphtali will be**

> humbled, but there will be a time in the future when
> Galilee of the Gentiles, which lies along the road that
> runs between the Jordan and the sea, will be filled with
> glory.
> The people who walk in darkness
> will see a great light.
> For those who live in a land of deep darkness,
> a light will shine. *Isaiah 9:1-2*

The middle and last parts of Isaiah pick up this theme of God's light that will transform the whole world through His people as they return from exile.

> "Arise, Jerusalem! Let your light shine for all to see.
> For the glory of the Lord rises to shine on you.
> Darkness as black as night covers all the nations of the
> earth,
> but the glory of the Lord rises and appears over you.
> All nations will come to your light;
> mighty kings will come to see your radiance."
> *Isaiah 60:1-3*

The Light of the Messiah

That promise in Isaiah, the light for all nations, is fulfilled in the person of Jesus. The first words of creation are, "Let there be light" (Genesis 1:3). The Word of God who was present in creation also lights our way in the darkness.

> The Word gave life to everything that was created,
> and his life brought light to everyone.
> The light shines in the darkness, and the darkness,
> can never extinguish it. *John 1:4-5*

Some could see that light in Jesus from His birth. When Simeon sees the infant Jesus in the temple, he breaks out in song.

"Sovereign Lord, now let your servant die in peace,
as you have promised.
I have seen your salvation,
which you have prepared for all people.
He is a light to reveal God to the nations,
and he is the glory of your people Israel! *Luke 2:29-32*

In His ministry Jesus announces to others that He is the light.

Jesus spoke to the people once more and said, "I am the light of the world. If you follow me, you won't have to walk in darkness, because you will have the light that leads to life." *John 8:12*

Light from the Lord begins and ends the Bible. The first words of creation are, "Let there be light" (Genesis 1:3). Almost the last words of the Bible tell of the new creation where "there will be no night there—no need for lamps or sun—for the Lord God will shine on them" (Revelation 22:5).

We especially long for that light from God when we are stumbling in the darkness. We don't know what the future holds. We cannot see the path before us. We remember all the times we thought we were on the right road only to end alone in the darkness.

Living in the Light

But by faith we walk in the light of Jesus that brings fellowship, forgiveness, and life.

This is the message we heard from Jesus and now declare to you: God is light, and there is no darkness in him at all. So we are lying if we say we have fellowship with God but go on living in spiritual darkness; we are not practicing the truth. But if we are living in the light, as God is in the light, then we have fellowship with each

other, and the blood of Jesus, his Son, cleanses us from all sin. *1 John 1:5-7*

As those living in the light of God through Jesus, we shine a light to help all those around us who are groping in darkness. Jesus tells us:

"You are the light of the world—like a city on a hilltop that cannot be hidden. No one lights a lamp and then puts it under a basket. Instead, a lamp is placed on a stand, where it gives light to everyone in the house. In the same way, let your good deeds shine out for all to see, so that everyone will praise your heavenly Father." *Matthew 5:14-16*

We live in a world of darkness. The news bombards us with stories and pictures of war, crime, violence, and disasters. Those who should lighten the load of others—parents, politicians, and even pastors—sometimes abuse and darken their lives. A world of falsehood, evil, and deception is crying for the light of the Lord. By remembering the pain of our own darkness and the joy of discovering the light, Jesus calls us to shine that light to everyone at every moment of the day.

For once you were full of darkness, but now you have light from the Lord. So live as people of light! For this light within you produces only what is good and right and true. *Ephesians 5:8*

Arise and shine, for your light has come!

For Reflection

1. What are some ways that you have walked in darkness?

2. How is our world walking in darkness?

3. How does the light of Jesus change us and our world?

Living the Messiah

1. Show the light of Christ to others by doing what is good and right and true.

2. Discuss with others in your church a way that all of you can bring light to a situation in your community.

Prayer

God of light, show us the way this day. Jesus, light of the world, may we walk in your light and shine that light for others to follow you.

DAY SEVEN:
NAME

For unto us a child is born, unto us a Son is given: and the government shall be upon His shoulder: and His name shall be called Wonderful, Counsellor, The Mighty God, The Everlasting Father, The Prince of Peace.
Isaiah 9:6

Most of us do not know what our names mean. They are just tags for people to call us. If we are named after a beloved relative, then our names help us recall them with fondness. In many cultures, including those of the Bible, names describe the character of those who hold them. Some societies even wait to name a child until their actions show what name they should receive.

Names mean something in the Bible. When they heard "Abraham," they thought "father." Isaac is "laughter." Joshua is "The Lord is salvation." Most important is the name of God, a name so sacred that many of God's people refused to say it out loud. Likely it was pronounced "Yahweh," but Jews substituted "The Lord" to avoid profaning the Name.

The Name of a Child

After proclaiming the great light that is to come, Isaiah links that light to the birth of a child who will govern God's people. Those in his day expected a king who would rule a restored Israel with justice and peace, however, the description of this child who will be king is so extravagant that one wonders how it can be applied to an Israelite king.

Perhaps those in Isaiah's time understood the name of this child as prophetic hyperbole. Early Christians who believed firmly in one God, came to see the parts of this name as apt descriptions of Jesus, the child born in Bethlehem.

All the names given to that child are rich in meaning. Jesus is the same name as Joshua—"The Lord is Salvation." Immanuel is "God with us." Christ is not a name but a title: "Messiah." But no name is as evocative as this muti-faceted name from Isaiah. Jesus truly has the name above all names (Philippians 2:9).

Wonderful Counselor

Although these words are separated in the text of *Messiah*, "wonderful" modifies "counselor." This child will be a wonderful counselor. Wonderful here means more than delightful or pleasing. It has the connotation of a wonder, that is, something beyond human ability or comprehension. The Bible uses the word to describe the actions of God, not human actions. This child to come will be a miraculous, supernatural counselor. His wisdom will come from above.

Counselor here is more than one who gives good advice. The word includes putting that advice into action. This counselor strategizes and accomplishes His purposes.

Jesus is the Wonderful Counselor. When He begins His ministry, people who know Him marvel at His wisdom.

> **He returned to Nazareth, his hometown. When he taught there in the synagogue, everyone was amazed and said, "Where does he get this wisdom and the power to do miracles?"** *Matthew 13:54*

Jesus channels the wisdom of God. That makes Jesus the source of all wisdom, the one who guides our lives with His miraculous strategy. He shows us the just path for our lives and the lives of all in our world. He reveals God's wonderful plan.

> **I want them to be encouraged and knit together by strong ties of love. I want them to have complete confidence that they understand God's mysterious plan, which is Christ himself. In him lie hidden all the treasures of wisdom and knowledge.** *Colossians 2:2-3*

> **But to those called by God to salvation, both Jews and Gentiles, Christ is the power of God and the wisdom of God.**
> **God has united you with Christ Jesus. For our benefit God made him to be wisdom itself. Christ made us right with God; he made us pure and holy, and he freed us from sin.** *1 Corinthians 1:24, 30*

What good news that God has not left us to run our own lives as best we can, but He has sent us His Wonderful Counselor!

Mighty God

The Bible often speaks of God as Almighty. God has all power. When He fights for His people, no one can stand against Him.

It is shocking, even approaching blasphemy, to refer to a human being as the Mighty God, yet this child to be born is to be God.

How can this be? How can a human being claim to be God? No wonder some accused Jesus of blasphemy when He claimed a special relationship with God as Father.

> **So the Jewish leaders tried all the harder to find a way to kill him. For he not only broke the Sabbath, he called God his Father, thereby making himself equal with God.** *John 5:18*

No human being should claim to be Almighty God, yet the early Christians clearly made that claim about Jesus.

> **In the beginning the Word already existed. The Word was with God, and the Word was God.** *John 1:1*

> **Christ is the visible image of the invisible God.** *Colossians 1:15*

> **For in Christ lives all the fullness of God in a human body.** *Colossians 2:9*

Christians believe that the baby in the manger in Bethlehem was the Messiah. What's more, we believe he was the Mighty God in the flesh. We are firm believers in only one God, but we see both the Father and the Son as God. Other scriptures and our own experience reveal the Holy Spirit as more than an influence from God, but as another person or manifestation of the Godhead. Not three gods, but one God in three persons. This is the mystery of the Trinity. We are led to that mystery in biblical passages like this that call a human child to be born, "Mighty God."

Everlasting Father

What might be even more of a mystery, or even more confusing, is to call this child to be born "the Everlasting Father." Jesus often calls God His Father, making a clear distinction between God the Father and God the Son. Yet He can also say, "The Father and I are one"

(John 10:30). If they are one, is the Son the Father? Can we call Jesus the Everlasting Father?

Yes, we can! Whatever we say about God the Father we can say about the human Jesus. Whatever we say about the human Jesus we can say about God the Father. The technical theological term for this is the "communication of idioms." This term reminds us that anything we say about God is an idiom, a metaphor. Human words cannot adequately describe God. The Father is not a literal father in the human sense. Neither is the Son a literal son. God the Father did not literally give birth to the Son. All these are word pictures that describe God as best we limited humans can understand.

However, the divine and human are so united in Jesus the Messiah that what we say about one we can say about the other. It is right to speak of God dying on the Cross. It is correct to say Jesus created the world. While this language might confuse some, it is theologically healthy. The child born in the manger is the Everlasting Father,

Prince of Peace

Shalom, peace, is the Hebrew word that everyone knows. It can be used as a greeting, a farewell, or a wish for someone's good health. The word means more than the absence of conflict. *Shalom* can refer to the ultimate harmony between God and humanity and among all people.

This promised child will bring reconciliation and loving relationship between God and humans.

> **Therefore, since we have been made right in God's sight by faith, we have peace with God because of what Jesus Christ our Lord has done for us.** *Romans 5:1*

Our rebellion against God has ended. Jesus has made peace by uniting the divine and human in the incarnation and by bringing us together with God through the cross. No longer are we estranged from our

Father, but He embraces us as His beloved children. We are at peace in His arms.

Jesus also brings peace to warring groups of people, removing the hatred we have toward those who are our enemies.

> **For he himself is our peace, who has made the two groups one and has destroyed the barrier, the dividing wall of hostility, by setting aside in his flesh the law with its commands and regulations. His purpose was to create in himself one new humanity out of the two, thus making peace, and in one body to reconcile both of them to God through the cross, by which he put to death their hostility. He came and preached peace to you who were far away and peace to those who were near.** *Ephesians 2:14-17 (NIV)*

His peace heals the hatred between Jew and Gentile. What's more it breaks all hostility between humans. No more wars between nations. No wars between men and women, Republicans and Democrats, liberal and conservative, young and old, settled and immigrants, one nation and another. Jesus is the Prince of Peace who enforces His peace on others, not by violence, but through sacrificial love.

These are all marvelous descriptions of the child who is to govern all people in justice. They are wonderful depictions of the Messiah, Jesus of Nazareth, but they are more than descriptions or names of Jesus. They are His name. One Name: Wonderful Counselor—Mighty God—Everlasting Father—Prince of Peace." That singular name reminds us that Jesus is the Name. He is all that God is.

For Reflection

1. Why are names so important in the Bible?

2. What is the significance of the Name of God?

3. Which of these descriptions of the Messiah do you find most surprising? Why?

Living the Messiah

1. Spend some time meditating on each of the descriptions of the child who is to come.

2. Work to make peace between people or groups who are at war with each other.

Prayer

God, we thank you for coming to us in a child. Jesus, we praise you for your wisdom, power, love, and peace. May everything we do glorify your matchless Name!

DAY EIGHT:
SHEPHERDS

There were shepherds abiding in the field, keeping watch over their flocks by night.

And lo, the angel of the Lord came upon them, and the glory of the Lord shone round about them, and they were sore afraid.

And the angel said unto them, Fear not; for, behold I bring you good tidings of great joy, which shall be to all people. For unto you is born this day in the city of David a Saviour, which is Christ the Lord.

And suddenly there was with the angel a multitude of the heavenly host praising God, and saying: Glory to God in the highest, and peace on earth, good will towards men.
Luke 2:8-11, 13-14

When I was growing up, every kid wanted to be a cowboy or cowgirl. Cowboys were ruggedly independent, fought for justice, and always defeated the bad guys. At least that's what they did in the movies and on television. The reality of being a cowboy was quite different. They moved from place to place, worked long hours in a grueling job, and lived in poverty. No wonder cowboys had a bad reputation as vagrants, drunks, and thieves.

Ordinary Shepherds

Shepherds were the cowboys of the Bible. On the one hand, they were idealized. After all, David the great king began as a shepherd. The best known psalm begins, "The Lord is my shepherd" (Psalm 23:1). When people called you a shepherd, they thought of the care of the Lord and the reign of his anointed king.

Or maybe not. In reality, shepherds often had a bad reputation. They were nomads, easily blamed for stealing and other criminal acts. They worked with dirty animals and carried the smell of sheep on their clothing. They were generally uneducated and from the lower rungs of society. Think of shepherds as lower than cowboys and more like fieldhands.

So it is amazing that the first group to hear of the birth of the Messiah is a group of shepherds in the fields. Or perhaps it is not so surprising; after all, the Lord has always cared for the poor and others despised by elite society. God promises to send a just king to rescue them.

> **He will rescue the poor when they cry to him;**
> **he will help the oppressed, who have no one to defend**
> **them.**
> **He feels pity for the weak and the needy,**
> **and he will rescue them.**
> **He will redeem them from oppression and violence,**
> **for their lives are precious to him.** *Psalm 72:12-14*

When Jesus begins His ministry, He targets the poor.

> **"The Spirit of the Lord is upon me,**
> **for he has anointed me to bring Good News to the poor."**
> *Luke 2:18, quoting Isaiah 61:1*

No wonder, then, that the good news of the birth of Jesus is told first to ordinary men doing a tough and thankless job. These are God's people.

Angels

The proclaimers of this good news are also amazing, first, one angel, then a host of angels. The angels of the Lord often bring good news in the Bible. An angel appears to Hagar promising her a child after Sarah had treated her harshly (Genesis 16:7-16). Angels encourage Jacob before he meets with Esau (Genesis 32:1). When Elijah is so discouraged that he wants to die, an angel feeds and strengthens him (1 Kings 19:4-9). An angel delivers Daniel from the mouth of the lions (Daniel 6:22).

Angels play a pivotal role in the life of Jesus, even before His birth. The angel Gabriel appears to Zechariah to tell him he and his wife Elizabeth will be the father and mother of John the Baptist (Luke 1:11-25). Gabriel announces the conception from the Holy Spirit to the virgin Mary (Luke 1:26-38). When Joseph is thinking of breaking his engagement to Mary, an angel of the Lord tells him the child is from the Holy Spirit (Matthew 1:18-25).

So angels now declare the birth of Jesus to the shepherds, first with one voice, then a host, an army of angels. The Bible often speaks of God as the "Lord of hosts" meaning the Lord of heaven's army. Think of what God can do with an angel army. He could violently force everyone to worship Him, but this army proclaims another way of conquering. This newborn is the Messiah, the one who will save the world through His gracious sacrifice.

No Fear, but Peace

When the angels appear, the shepherds are afraid. This is the usual reaction to angels in the Bible. That may seem strange to us who think of angels as cherubs—cute babies with wings. Biblical angels are frightening because they come from the throne of the Almighty God. They carry the terrifying glory of God with them.

So the angel says, "Fear not." Angels are not only scary in themselves, but they sometimes bring words of harsh punishment from God. Not this time! This angel has "good tidings of great joy." He broadcasts the best news ever heard. Messiah, the Savior that God's people have been awaiting for ages, has been born nearby. This joyful news is not just for Israel as God's people. It is for all people.

And as we saw in the previous part of *Messiah*, the one to come is the Prince of Peace. It is no surprise that these angels proclaim "peace on earth" when He is born.

Angels announce His birth, but they are not the last to share this good news.

> **When the angels had left them and gone into heaven, the shepherds said to one another, "Let's go to Bethlehem and see this thing that has happened, which the Lord has told us about."**
> **So they hurried off and found Mary and Joseph, and the baby, who was lying in the manger. When they had seen him, they spread the word concerning what had been told them about this child, and all who heard it were amazed at what the shepherds said to them. But Mary treasured up all these things and pondered them in her heart. The shepherds returned, glorifying and praising God for all the things they had heard and seen, which were just as they had been told.** *Luke 2:15-20 (NIV)*

Although despised by some, these ordinary shepherds are the first evangelists in the New Testament. They joyfully share the news the angels brought, news they confirmed with their own eyes.

For Reflection

1. Why do you think God targets ordinary people to hear the good news?

2. How do you picture angels? Are they frightening to you? Why or why not?

3. Why do you think God sent a host of angels? Wouldn't one have been enough?

Living the Messiah

1. Look for the presence of angels in your life today.

2. By word or action, share the good news of the birth of Jesus.

Prayer

Lord of all the angels of heaven, thank you for this great news of the birth of Jesus, our Savior. Fill us with the joy of that news so it will overflow from our lives to others.

DAY NINE:
KING

Rejoice greatly, O daughter of Zion! Shout, O daughter of Jerusalem! Behold, thy King cometh unto thee! He is the righteous Saviour, and He shall speak peace unto the heathen. *Zechariah 9:9-10*

"If we'd only elect him, then we could recover the greatness we once had."

"When she gets into office, then we will have justice and peace."

We've heard these kinds of statements from others. We may have even said them ourselves. We vote in hopes that our candidate for mayor or governor or president will make things better. Happy days will be here again!

Yet we've also been deeply disappointed in those whom we have elected. They seldom turn out to be the liberator or protector we envisioned. Our form of government limits the power of those we elect. But what if they had complete power? What if they were kings? Would they then be able to do all we hoped for?

God as King

Israel's first experience with a great king was with the King of Egypt. Pharoah, with the help of Joseph (and the Lord), saved Israel and his family from starvation (Genesis 46:1-47:31). But later there arose a Pharoah who did not remember Joseph, so he enslaved Israel (Exodus 1:8-11). In slavery, God's people cry out to Him. Eventually the Lord delivers them by sending the plagues through Moses and drowning Pharoah's army in the Red Sea.

After such a terrible experience with Pharoah, one would think that a king would be the last thing the Israelites would want. Yet, after they eventually enter the Promised Land, they ask for a king!

> **Finally, all the elders of Israel met at Ramah to discuss the matter with Samuel. "Look," they told him, "you are now old, and your sons are not like you. Give us a king to judge us like all the other nations have."**
> **Samuel was displeased with their request and went to the Lord for guidance. "Do everything they say to you," the Lord replied, "for they are rejecting me, not you. They don't want me to be their king any longer."** *1 Samuel 8:5-7*

The Lord was King before there was an Israel, King from creation. Had Israel forgotten that He was their King? That seems unlikely, since they had a visual reminder of His reign in the Ark of the Covenant, in the Tabernacle, and in the Temple. Later biblical writers speak of God ruling from His throne, the Mercy Seat on top of the Ark.

> **The Lord is king! Let the nations tremble! He sits on his throne between the cherubim. Let the whole earth quake!** *Psalm 99:1*

> **And Hezekiah prayed this prayer before the Lord: "O Lord of Heaven's Armies, God of Israel, you are enthroned between the mighty cherubim! You alone are God of all the kingdoms of the earth. You alone created the heavens and the earth."** *Isaiah 37:15-16*

God's people are not content with the Lord as their only King. They want a human ruler like the other nations.

Kings of Judah and Israel

So the Lord allows them to have kings. While some of them are good kings, God's people are soon disappointed in their kings. The Lord himself is greatly angered at the kings that led the people to worship other gods. Yet God always holds out the hope that there will be kings who bring justice and turn the people's hearts back to Him. Those kings realize that the Lord is the true King who rules with justice.

In spite of all his sins, David is the model king. He always points the people to the Lord as their King (see Psalms 5:2, 24:7-10, 95:3, 145:1). That faithfulness is why God promises the line of Davidic kings will continue.

> **"Furthermore, the Lord declares that he will make a house for you—a dynasty of kings! For when you die and are buried with your ancestors, I will raise up one of your descendants, your own offspring, and I will make his kingdom strong. He is the one who will build a house— a temple—for my name. And I will secure his royal throne forever. I will be his father, and he will be my son. If he sins, I will correct and discipline him with the rod, like any father would do. But my favor will not be taken from him as I took it from Saul, whom I removed from your sight. Your house and your kingdom will continue before me for all time, and your throne will be secure forever."** *2 Samuel 7:11-16*

Jesus as King

So Zechariah and other prophets speak of a king who is to come, one from David's line who will rule in justice and peace. He will reign not only over Israel, but over all nations.

Before Jesus is born, Gabriel tells Mary that He will be given the throne of David and that His reign will never end (Luke 2:31-33). After He is born, the wise men come to find the King of the Jews (Matthew 2:2). Jesus is crucified because He claims to be a king (Luke 23:1).

This verse from Zechariah 9 is quoted when Jesus makes his Triumphal Entry into Jerusalem.

> **Jesus found a young donkey and rode on it, fulfilling the**
> **prophecy that said:**
> **"Don't be afraid, people of Jerusalem.**
> **Look, your King is coming,**
> **riding on a donkey's colt."**
> **His disciples didn't understand at the time that this was**
> **a fulfillment of prophecy. But after Jesus entered into his**
> **glory, they remembered what had happened and realized**
> **that these things had been written about him.**
> *John 12:14-16 (see also Matthew 21:4-5)*

What great news for Israel! After centuries of disenchantment with their kings, after exile, after being conquered by nation after nation, their True King has come. What great news for all the nations of the world! No matter how good or how bad their leaders are, the Lord Jesus is the King who brings peace. What great news to us! Our King is a flesh-and-blood Savior and yet He is also the God who has ruled since creation. Rejoice greatly!

For Reflection

1. What comes to mind when you think of "king"? Does the word give you hope or frighten you? Why?

2. Why was Israel not content to have God alone as their king? Why do we keep expecting politicians to make everything better?

3. What kind of King is Jesus? How does He rule?

Living the Messiah

1. As you pray, fall face down and picture God on His heavenly throne, ruling the universe.

2. Since Jesus the King brings peace, live in peace with others today.

Prayer

King of the Universe, we fall down before you. Jesus, Savior and King, rule our lives this day so that we might show your peace to others.

DAY TEN:
HEALING

Then shall the eyes of the blind be opened, and the ears of the deaf unstopped. Then shall the lame man leap as an hart, and the tongue of the dumb shall sing. *Isaiah 35:5-6*

"It's the new normal."

That's a phrase I'm tired of hearing from my doctor. It means she can do nothing to help my aches and pains. I just have to learn to live with them.

But there are disabilities that are heavy burdens to bear. Blindness affects every aspect of your life. To be completely deaf is to be cut off from much of the world. When you must use a wheelchair to be mobile, it limits what you can do. If one cannot speak, it is extremely frustrating. I admire those who deal with these and other physical challenges.

There are some disorders that are completely debilitating. And there are ailments that are terminal. One cannot live for long with them. Whether it be daily aches or serious disabilities or incurable diseases, there's something not right about suffering, pain, and death. This cannot be the way God intended life to be.

The Blind See

So Isaiah looks forward to the time when all illnesses are cured. His description of that time reminds us of the ministry of Jesus. Jesus was a healer. He completely cured those who had been told to "live with it." He gave them new life. Jesus gave sight to the blind, even to a man born blind.

> **As he passed by, he saw a man blind from birth. And his disciples asked him, "Rabbi, who sinned, this man or his parents, that he was born blind?" Jesus answered, "It was not that this man sinned, or his parents, but that the works of God might be displayed in him. We must work the works of him who sent me while it is day; night is coming, when no one can work. As long as I am in the world, I am the light of the world." Having said these things, he spit on the ground and made mud with the saliva. Then he anointed the man's eyes with the mud and said to him, "Go, wash in the pool of Siloam" (which means Sent). So he went and washed and came back seeing. *John 9:1-7 (ESV)***

One thing that frustrates disabled people is that other people look past them or see them as a category, not as an individual. The disciples see the man who is blind as a theological question. Jesus sees him as one who will receive the power of God. What a wonderful thing to see for the first time!

Later in the story, Jesus confronts those who are not physically blind but who will not see the powerful work of God in Jesus.

> **Then Jesus told him, "I entered this world to render judgment—to give sight to the blind and to show those who think they see that they are blind."**

> **Some Pharisees who were standing nearby heard him and asked, "Are you saying we're blind?"**
> **"If you were blind, you wouldn't be guilty," Jesus replied. "But you remain guilty because you claim you can see."**
> *John 9:39-41*

The Deaf Hear, The Mute Speak

Helen Keller, who was blind and deaf, thought deafness was more challenging, saying "Blindness separates people from things; deafness separates people from people." Jesus healed the deaf as well as the blind.

> **A deaf man with a speech impediment was brought to him, and the people begged Jesus to lay his hands on the man to heal him.**
> **Jesus led him away from the crowd so they could be alone. He put his fingers into the man's ears. Then, spitting on his own fingers, he touched the man's tongue. Looking up to heaven, he sighed and said, "Ephphatha," which means, "Be opened!" Instantly the man could hear perfectly, and his tongue was freed so he could speak plainly!** *Mark 7:32-35*

This man had friends who loved him and wanted him to be able to communicate better with them. By restoring his hearing and speech, Jesus gives him a closer relationship with his community.

The Lame Walk

Those who cannot walk know the distress of being shut out of many places, even in our day of government mandates for access of those with disabilities. In Bible times, those who could not walk often could not work and were in danger of starvation. Still, there is a greater need than being cured of paralysis.

Some people brought to him a paralyzed man on a mat. Seeing their faith, Jesus said to the paralyzed man, "Be encouraged, my child! Your sins are forgiven."

But some of the teachers of religious law said to themselves, "That's blasphemy! Does he think he's God?"

Jesus knew what they were thinking, so he asked them, "Why do you have such evil thoughts in your hearts? Is it easier to say 'Your sins are forgiven,' or 'Stand up and walk'? So I will prove to you that the Son of Man has the authority on earth to forgive sins." Then Jesus turned to the paralyzed man and said, "Stand up, pick up your mat, and go home!"

And the man jumped up and went home! Fear swept through the crowd as they saw this happen. And they praised God for giving humans such authority. *Matthew 9:2-8*

Why Did Jesus Heal?

Jesus healed because people needed healing. He felt compassion toward those who had to live with blindness, deafness, and paralysis, but He did not heal all the sick. Why not?

Because his purpose was not to eradicate disease in His lifetime. His purpose was to announce that the Kingdom of God had come. Isaiah looks forward to the day when the just king comes and brings healing to the world. Jesus is that Messiah, the King who brings salvation and righteousness.

That's why the people who see the healing of the paralyzed man praise God for the authority Jesus has. Messiah has the power from God to make all things right. In the beginning, God did not intend for humans to know sickness. Messiah heals. God did not intend for humans to sin. Messiah has the authority to forgive sin.

Now that Jesus the Messiah has come, the blind see, the deaf hear, the lame leap, the mute sing praise. Now that Jesus the Messiah is here, sins are forgiven. The Lord is working through Jesus the Messiah to make things the way He intended for them to be from the beginning. In the new heavens and earth,

> **I heard a loud shout from the throne, saying, "Look, God's home is now among his people! He will live with them, and they will be his people. God himself will be with them. He will wipe every tear from their eyes, and there will be no more death or sorrow or crying or pain. All these things are gone forever."** *Revelation 21:3-4*

We will no longer have to live with disabilities, pain, sin, and death. We will live with the Messiah, the source of life. We will see God, hear His voice, walk with Him, and sing His praises forever.

For Reflection

1. Which would you find most challenging, to lose your sight, your hearing, your speech, or your ability to walk? Why?

2. What is worse, to be physically blind or spiritually blind? Why?

3. What does healing have to do with authority?

Living the Messiah

1. Take a walk in silence and open your eyes and your ears to what God is doing around you.

2. Remind yourself to see people with disabilities.

Prayer

Lord Jesus, open our eyes so we may see you at work. Open our ears to hear your voice. May we walk with you this day? Open our mouths to speak your gracious words to others and to praise your Name. Come quickly, Lord, and make all things right.

DAY ELEVEN:
SHEPHERD

He shall feed His flock like a shepherd, and He shall gather the lambs with His arm, and carry them in His bosom, and gently lead those that are with young. *Isaiah 40:11*

Sheep are dumb. That's the stereotype I learned, but those who raise sheep say they are quite intelligent. Their reputation for getting lost is not because they are mindless, but because of two other characteristics of sheep. Sheep flock together and they are easily led. Perhaps that's why the Bible often portrays God's people as sheep.

God as Shepherd

In Genesis, Jacob describes God as his shepherd (Genesis 48:15). Abraham, Isaac, and Jacob were shepherds, so they knew what it took to look after sheep. A good shepherd leads his sheep to water and to pastures where they can graze. The best known psalm speaks of God that way.

> **The Lord is my shepherd;**
> **I have all that I need.**

He lets me rest in green meadows;
he leads me beside peaceful streams.
He renews my strength.
He guides me along right paths,
bringing honor to his name. *Psalm 23:1-3*

With the Lord as our Shepherd, we have all that we need. We are free from thirst, from hunger, and from danger.

The Lord acted as a shepherd to His people when He led them out of Egypt in the Exodus and provided water and food for them in the desert.

But he led his own people like a flock of sheep,
guiding them safely through the wilderness. *Psalm 78:52*

Later, when God's people turn against Him, he sends them into exile. Even there, He does not abandon them, but promises to be their Shepherd and lead them back to their land.

"For this is what the Sovereign Lord says: I myself will search and find my sheep. I will be like a shepherd looking for his scattered flock. I will find my sheep and rescue them from all the places where they were scattered on that dark and cloudy day. I will bring them back home to their own land of Israel from among the peoples and nations. I will feed them on the mountains of Israel and by the rivers and in all the places where people live. Yes, I will give them good pastureland on the high hills of Israel. There they will lie down in pleasant places and feed in the lush pastures of the hills." *Ezekiel 34:11-14*

The Lord shepherds His people at all times, leading them from Egypt, returning them after the exile, and caring for us each day. We are so familiar with the idea of the Lord as Shepherd that we may miss the power of this metaphor. Shepherds live with the sheep. They feed them, call them by name, and protect them. A good shepherd is gentle with newborn lambs, feeding them by hand. The portrait of the Lord here is not of a distant God thundering condemnation, but of one who has an intimate relationship with His people, caring for them with His own hands.

Jesus as Shepherd

That is the kind of care Jesus provides for us. Echoing all the Old Testament references to the Lord as Shepherd, Jesus describes Himself this way:

> **"I am the good shepherd; I know my own sheep, and they know me, just as my Father knows me and I know the Father. So I sacrifice my life for the sheep. I have other sheep, too, that are not in this sheepfold. I must bring them also. They will listen to my voice, and there will be one flock with one shepherd."** *John 10:14-16*

The good shepherd knows His sheep. Jesus knows us. He knows us better than we know ourselves, inside and out. That knowledge is personal and intimate. He knows us and He still loves us! He feeds and protects, even at the cost of His life.

Jesus calls His sheep to follow Him and be one flock. The individualism of our culture makes us prone to think of Jesus as our personal Savior, perhaps even our private Savior—"It's all about me and Jesus." But the Good Shepherd calls the whole flock to follow Him. Jesus never intended church to be optional, only needed for our individual spiritual life. We are in this together with others. And He never intended the church to be divisive and exclusive. He invites all who will follow the Shepherd to be His sheep.

It's significant that the most popular image of Jesus found in early churches and catacombs is not the baby in the manger or the Savior on the cross. It is Jesus as the Good Shepherd carrying a young lamb across His shoulder. Isaiah says, "He shall gather the lambs with His arm, and carry them in His bosom." He is gentle with us who are young and vulnerable, carrying us when we can no longer go on.

I've never been a shepherd, but to tell the truth, it sounds boring. The sheep have to be watered and fed every day. You have to look for the lost sheep every day. The dailiness of it all would wear me out. The one who is "God with us" is the Lord who is our shepherd, and He is never too tired or bored to care for us, and meet all our needs.

We are Sheep

The Lord is our shepherd. That makes us sheep.

Who wants to be a sheep?

We want to be lions that rule the jungle. We want to be wolves that prey on others. There's a football team called the Rams but none called the Lambs.

Jesus calls us to be His sheep. What do sheep do? They drink. They eat. They follow. We live in a time obsessed with leadership. We think everyone should be trained to be a leader, but Jesus is more concerned with followship. Sheep flock together. So should we. Sheep are easily led. So we should be quick to follow our Shepherd.

But we easily follow others and get lost. More on that later in *Messiah*.

For Reflection

1. If you were a shepherd, what would you like or dislike about the job?

2. What does it cost God to be a shepherd to us? What does it cost Jesus?

3. Who might be the "other sheep" whom Jesus mentions? How can we help Him find those sheep?

Living the Messiah

1. Find a picture of Jesus as the Good Shepherd. Meditate on Him as you view that picture.

2. Talk to someone about Jesus as Shepherd. Share your insights and listen to theirs.

Prayer

Jesus, Great Shepherd, hold us gently in your arms this day. Feed us. Protect us. Gather us together with others so we might be one flock.

DAY TWELVE:
REST

Come unto Him, all ye that labor, come unto Him ye that are heavy laden, and He will give you rest. Take His yoke upon you, and learn of Him, for He is meek and lowly of heart, and ye shall find rest unto your souls. His yoke is easy, and His burthen is light. *Matthew 11:28-30*

How does your day begin?

The alarm wakes you from a restless sleep. You stumble into the bathroom to get ready for the day. Then you wake the kids and (with great effort) get them off to school. You choke down a quick breakfast, then go to the car to fight the traffic to get to work. On the way, you make a mental list of the five important tasks you have that day. When you get to the job, you find that someone has given you three urgent projects to complete before you can get to the five important ones.

It's only 9 AM and you are already exhausted.

How can you get some rest? Maybe a vacation will help. Time off from your usual responsibilities will revive you, but vacations are a strain, particularly if you have a family. There's the planning, the packing, the drive or the flight. You are away from your pillow and bed and routine. When you get home, there's the unpacking, the wash, and the bills to pay. You need a rest from your vacation.

Heavy Load

Almost everyone I know needs some rest. We are weary to our bones. Jesus speaks to people who need rest. Most of those who first heard Him were subsistence farmers or day laborers. They knew what hard work was like. They had a work week much longer than ours. Like us, they were more than physically tired. They were burdened, loaded down.

Think of the loads we carry. Family burdens. Your last daughter is two years from college and (as much as you love her) you are looking forward to an empty nest. Then your mother has a fall and has to come and live with you. Work burdens. For years I was a teacher. Each semester we received news of our teaching load. It was aptly named. Sometimes I even had an overload. We all know the burden of overtime we did not choose. Financial burdens. We think we are finally out of the hole only to have a storm cause costly damage to our house that insurance does not cover. Then there are the burdens of the world that we take on—politics, wars, and causes.

Heavier than all this is the load of sin, shame, and guilt.

> **My guilt overwhelms me—**
> **it is a burden too heavy to bear.** *Psalm 38:4*

We are burdened with regret. "If only I had done this. If only I could overcome this addiction. If only I had known better."

Who can lighten these overwhelming loads? Sometimes well-meaning church leaders make things worse, not better. They multiply church meetings, programs, seminars, and ministries, give us more than we can do and make us guilty for not doing enough. Jesus spoke of some not-so-well-meaning religious leaders who put loads on people.

> **"The teachers of religious law and the Pharisees are the official interpreters of the law of Moses. So practice and obey whatever they tell you, but don't follow their example. For they don't practice what they teach. They crush people with unbearable religious demands and never lift a finger to ease the burden."** *Matthew 23:2-4*

Some of us know the crushing weight of legalism and perfectionism. I grew up with Christians who prayed, "And when we have done all that we can do, give us a home with you in heaven." That prayer weighed on my conscience. How could I ever do "all that I can"? And if I could not, then would there be no heaven for me?

Easy Yoke

Jesus promises rest. Messiah gives release from our weight of guilt.

> **He personally carried our sins
> in his body on the cross
> so that we can be dead to sin
> and live for what is right.** *1 Peter 2:24*

Jesus carries the load of sin, shame, and guilt so that we no longer have to carry it. He gives us rest from the impossible burden of perfectionism. We rest in our right standing with God because of what Jesus did on the cross. Jesus promises more than just rest from our sin. He promises rest from all the many tasks and worries that burden us. How?

He invites us to take on a yoke. A yoke is a heavy wooden bar that connects two work animals to the plow or other load they carry. How can being yoked be rest? It sounds like work that only strong animals can do!

But Jesus says His yoke is easy and His burden is light. How? Keep in mind that the yoke binds two animals together. When Jesus tells us to take His yoke upon us; He is agreeing to pull the load with us. And He is so much stronger! He carries our load of sin. He takes away the weight of our worries.

> **Don't worry about anything; instead, pray about everything. Tell God what you need, and thank him for all he has done. Then you will experience God's peace, which exceeds anything we can understand. His peace will guard your hearts and minds as you live in Christ Jesus.** *Philippians 4:6-7*

> **Throw all your worry on him, because he cares for you.** *2 Peter 5:7 (ISV)*

The secret of the easy yoke is that Jesus is pulling with us, He shares the load. What does that mean when we reflect on the challenges of our lives? It means we do not bear responsibility for our sin; Jesus has forgiven us completely. Feeling guilty and ashamed does not help. Yes, we have the ability to respond to the grace of God in Christ, but we no longer have the burden of perfectionism or of doing "all that we can do." Jesus takes care of that.

What about family? Yes, we have duties as spouses, parents, and children, but there are times when we cannot make everything right for those we love. What we can do is to raise them up to God through Jesus in prayer, knowing that He alone knows what is best for them and that He loves them more than we do.

And our jobs? Yes, we give honest effort each day to earn our livelihood, except our worth is not tied to our titles or accomplishments. Jesus is with us on the job, giving us wisdom and energy to work not just for the boss but for Him (Colossians 3:23).

Financial stress?

"So don't worry about these things, saying, 'What will we eat? What will we drink? What will we wear?' These things dominate the thoughts of unbelievers, but your heavenly Father already knows all your needs. Seek the Kingdom of God above all else, and live righteously, and he will give you everything you need." *Matthew 6:31-33*

Finding Rest

If Jesus gives us this marvelous promise of rest, then why are we so tired? Might it be because we refuse to be yoked to Him? We want to run our own lives. We will not let go of our burdens because we want to do things our way.

This is what the Sovereign Lord,
the Holy One of Israel, says:
"Only in returning to me
and resting in me will you be saved.
In quietness and confidence is your strength."
But you would have none of it. *Isaiah 30:15*

We must surrender our desire to be the savior of our family or business or the world. We must accept the rest the Savior offers us. In the traditional wording of Psalm 23, the Lord "makes us lie down in green pastures." We simply need to let go, trust the Lord, lie down, and take our rest. Take His yoke and learn.

For Reflection

1. What tires you out the most? Why?

2. What does Jesus do as the one yoked to us?

3. Why would we refuse to rest? What does that say about us?

Living the Messiah

1. Take a day as a Sabbath to intentionally rest. Let Jesus do your work that day.

2. Provide rest for someone else by doing part of their job.

Prayer

Meek and lowly Jesus, give us rest this day. May we trust every part of our lives to your work for us, knowing that you take all our burdens away.

DAY THIRTEEN:
LAMB

Behold the Lamb of God that taketh away the sin of the world. *John 1:29*

It's hard to imagine anything more cute than a baby lamb; they look soft and helpless, Remember that for those who raised sheep in biblical times and today, lambs are livestock. They represent wealth. They might even save your family from starvation.

Lambs. Innocent and valuable. That may be why they were important as sacrifices.

Sacrificial Lambs

The first acceptable sacrifice made to God in the Bible is a lamb. Abel offers his best lambs as a gift to God (Genesis 4:4). When the Lord tells Abraham to offer his son Isaac, he and Isaac make the journey to the place of sacrifice. Along the way, Isaac asks a suggestive question.

And Isaac said to his father Abraham, "My father!" And he said, "Here I am, my son." He said, "Behold, the fire and the wood, but where is the lamb for a burnt

offering?" Abraham said, "God will provide for himself the lamb for a burnt offering, my son." So they went both of them together. *Genesis 22:7-8 (ESV)*

Later, God spares Isaac and provides a ram (not a lamb) as a sacrifice, prompting Abraham to name the place, "The Lord will provide" (Genesis 22:9-14).

At the first Passover, when the Lord rescues Israel by sending the death angel against the firstborn of the Egyptians, the Israelites are spared by placing the blood of lambs around their doorposts (Exodus 12:1-30). The lamb itself is eaten by the family in a ritual still practiced by observant Jews. Later, Israel's priests are instructed to offer one lamb in the morning and one in the evening on the altar of the Lord (Exodus 29:38-42). Other lambs are to be sacrificed in a variety of offerings (See Leviticus 9:3, 12:6-8, 14:10-25, 23:12-20).

Why Sacrifice?

The very idea of killing a defenseless lamb is offensive to many. Why would a God of love not only permit such a practice but require it?

Before we answer that, note that the Old Testament had strict rules about the humane killing of animals, whether for sacrifice or for food (see Leviticus 17). Many today who are appalled at the idea of killing a lamb for sacrifice eat meat that is slaughtered in an inhumane fashion.

But why animal sacrifice? This question is not answered directly in the Bible, but there are hints. First, sacrifices to the Lord are not like pagan sacrifices. Those who worshipped other gods thought that the sacrifices fed the god. The Lord does not need sacrifices to survive.

Instead, animal sacrifices are in some ways substitutes for human sacrifice. Sin has so separated us from God that we owe our lives to pay for sin. Instead of requiring that, God allows animal deaths as a substitute. Another way of saying this is that the horror we rightly feel at the bloody death of these innocent animals reminds us of the dire consequences of sin. These sacrifices were God's gracious way of covering their sin.

Jesus as the Lamb

With that in mind, to call Jesus "the Lamb of God that taketh away the sin of the world" is profoundly evocative. When John the Baptist comes, some think he is the Messiah. He tells them he is not, but he is there to point to one greater than himself.

> **The next day John saw Jesus coming toward him and said, "Look! The Lamb of God who takes away the sin of the world! He is the one I was talking about when I said, 'A man is coming after me who is far greater than I am, for he existed long before me.' I did not recognize him as the Messiah, but I have been baptizing with water so that he might be revealed to Israel." *John 1:29-31***

Jesus is the lamb of God. What does that mean? It means He is the lamb that is sacrificed to God, but it also means that He is the lamb from God. That is, Jesus in a fuller way reflects the confident statement of Abraham that "the Lord will provide a lamb for the sacrifice."

God gives what God requires—a perfect offering for sin. Jesus as the Lamb of God embodies all the lambs that had ever been sacrificed for sin, including the Passover lambs.

> **Christ, our Passover Lamb, has been sacrificed for us.**
> *1 Corinthians 5:7*

Just as the blood of the lamb saved God's people from the death angel, so this Lamb of God saves the world from death.

It is the blood of Jesus as the Lamb of God that gave those previous lambs the power to forgive sin. The effects of his atoning sacrifice stretch into the past as well as into the present and future.

> **For God presented Jesus as the sacrifice for sin. People are made right with God when they believe that Jesus sacrificed his life, shedding his blood. This sacrifice shows that God was being fair when he held back and did not punish those who sinned in times past, for he was looking ahead and including them in what he would do in this present time. God did this to demonstrate his righteousness, for he himself is fair and just, and he makes sinners right in his sight when they believe in Jesus.** *Romans 3:25-26*

God is fair in condemning sin and He is fair in making sinners right with Him, because He provides the offering—His only Son—for the atoning sacrifice.

That sacrifice can also be thought of as a ransom. By turning against God, humans embraced evil and fell under its power. It is as if we were kidnapped and held for ransom. God breaks the power of sin through Jesus. As the Lamb of God, He is the redemption price for our liberation.

> **For you know that God paid a ransom to save you from the empty life you inherited from your ancestors. And it was not paid with mere gold or silver, which lose their value. It was the precious blood of Christ, the sinless, spotless Lamb of God. God chose him as your ransom long before the world began, but now in these last days he has been revealed for your sake.** *1 Peter 1:18-20*

Messiah is full of sheep imagery. Shepherds hear the announcement of the birth of Jesus. Jesus as Messiah is the great shepherd, caring for us as His sheep. He also is the innocent, spotless lamb of God who takes away the sins of the world.

Behold the Lamb!

For Reflection

1. What picture comes to your mind when you think of a lamb? How does that picture relate to Jesus?

2. How do you feel about animal sacrifices? Why would God demand them?

3. How does Jesus as a sacrifice show the fairness or justice of God?

Living the Messiah

1. In gratitude for the sacrifice of the Lamb of God, give up something for God.

2. Sacrificially give to someone in need.

Prayer

Lamb of God, we praise you in gratitude for your great sacrifice for us. Like the first disciples may we follow you wherever you lead, offering all that we are to you.

DAY FOURTEEN:
REJECTED

He was despised and rejected of men, a man of sorrows, and acquainted with grief. *Isaiah 53:3*

"Don't bite the hand that feeds you."

The phrase originally referred to dogs, but came to be a metaphor for human ingratitude. We have all had the experience of helping someone, only to have them turn on us, "bite the hand," and sometimes chew vigorously.

I think of a young man that my wife and I went out of our way to help. We found him a place to stay. We had him over to our house for meals. We listened sympathetically to his struggles. We worked to find him a job. Then another job (when he lost that one). We prayed for him (and continue to do so). After a while, he left town and moved to another state. When we next heard from those who knew him, they told us how bitter he was toward us because of the way we mistreated him.

Such experiences can keep us from helping others. To use another dog metaphor, "Once bitten, twice shy." Why would we help someone who will reject our help?

One of the great mysteries of the Bible is why anyone would reject the love of God. God so loved that he gave His only Son. Yet when that Son became flesh and lived among us, many of those who knew Him rejected Him. How could they reject the Messiah, the Savior, the Shepherd, and the Lamb of God who takes away the sins of the world?

Rejected Jesus

There was much rejoicing when Jesus entered the world. Mary, Joseph, shepherds, wise men, Simeon, and Anna all praised this new king. When Jesus began His ministry, all spoke well of Him, but that soon changed. Before long, those He came to save, even those who should have known Him best, turned against Him. Who was it that rejected Jesus?

- **HIS FAMILY.**

The brothers of Jesus did not believe in Him (John 7:5). It would be hard to believe that your brother was the Messiah. Early in the ministry of Jesus, His family tried to take Him home because they thought He was out of His mind (Mark 3:21). Later, two of his brothers, James and Jude, came to faith and became leaders in the early church.

- **HIS HOMETOWN**

Jesus has a homecoming, speaking in the synagogue in Nazareth. At first everyone praises Him as the local boy who made good, but Jesus turns from telling of good news to the poor to reminding those in Nazareth that God also sent prophets and healing to foreigners. That infuriates them so much that they unsuccessfully try to kill Jesus, threatening to push Him over a cliff. This episode causes Jesus to say that no prophet is accepted in his own hometown (Luke 7:14-30).

- ### GENTILES AND SAMARITANS

Since Jesus promises good news to all, one might think that those outside of Israel welcomed Him. Instead, on one occasion, after witnessing Jesus casting a demon out of a man, the Gerasenes beg Jesus to leave their land (Luke 8:26-37). Those in a Samaritan village will not even let Jesus and the disciples set foot there (Luke 9:51-56).

- ### RELIGIOUS LEADERS

The Pharisees, Sadducees, priests, and experts in the Law generally opposed Jesus from early in His ministry. That opposition intensified, leading them to hand Jesus over to the Roman authorities for crucifixion. Jesus predicted their hostile actions (Luke 9:22).

- ### THE DISCIPLES

Surely those who were closest to Jesus and who spent so much time learning from Him would not reject Him. Yet it is one of the twelve apostles, Judas, who betrays Him to death (Matthew 26:14-16). Peter denies Jesus three times (Matthew 26:69-75, John 18:15-27). All of the twelve abandon Jesus when He is arrested in Gethsemane (Mark 14:50, Matthew 26:56).

Why Reject Jesus?

Since Jesus came to save the world, why would those who saw Him with their own eyes reject His salvation?

There are many reasons. One is familiarity. It would be hard to believe your brother or the carpenter who helped build your house was the Messiah. Some Samaritans believe in Jesus (John 4:39-42). Others reject Him out of prejudice toward Jews (Luke 9:51-56). Gentiles like the wise men and a Roman soldier believe in Jesus (Matt. 8:5-13; Luke 7:1-10), but some refuse Him out of fear of His power (Luke 9:51-56).

There are two prominent Jewish leaders—Nicodemus and Joseph of Arimathea—who are secret disciples of Jesus and bury Him with respect (John 3:1-12, 7:50-52, 19:38-42). Most of the leaders criticized Jesus for breaking their understanding of the Law, for example by healing on the Sabbath. Their opposition grows more heated when they perceive that Jesus is claiming to be in some way equal to God. At His trial, they accuse Him of many things—planning to destroying the temple, blasphemy, and rebellion against Rome (Mark 15:3). Their hatred of Jesus goes beyond differences in Bible interpretation. Some of it is rooted in jealousy (Matthew 27:18).

Peter denies Jesus and the disciples flee Gethsemane out of fear that they too might be crucified. The motivations of Judas for his betrayal are murky, but greed was part of it (John 12:6, Matthew 26:15). Except for Judas, the apostles all return to Jesus after the crucifixion.

Many cannot follow Jesus because they cannot accept His teachings. When He speaks of His disciples eating His body and drinking His blood, many of them leave.

> **At this point many of his disciples turned away and deserted him. Then Jesus turned to the Twelve and asked, "Are you also going to leave?"**
> **Simon Peter replied, "Lord, to whom would we go? You have the words that give eternal life. We believe, and we know you are the Holy One of God."** *John 6:66-69*

The teaching that almost everyone in His day could not accept was when Jesus spoke of the Messiah as one who suffers and dies. From many verses in the Old Testament, they knew that the Messiah would reign as a king like David. He would conquer their enemies and set His people free. He would rule with justice and bring peace. How could He do this if He were put to death as a criminal?

But what about these words from *Messiah*, quoting Isaiah 53? Surely they speak of one who would be rejected, punished, and killed. As we will see, those in the time of Jesus did not think these words were about the Messiah but about another suffering servant, perhaps the nation of Israel itself.

So the very opposition to Jesus confirmed that He was not the Messiah they expected.

Reacting to Rejection

How does Jesus react to rejection? With anger and vengeance?

No. He does warn of the consequences of rejecting Him and His message of love.

> **"And anyone who rejects me is rejecting God, who sent me."** *Luke 10:16*

Jesus warns his listeners to follow the instruction of the teachers of religious law but not to follow their actions. His words against these leaders who reject Him are harsh (Matthew 23:1-36), but He says them out of compassion for His people, ending with this cry.

> **"O Jerusalem, Jerusalem, the city that kills the prophets and stones God's messengers! How often I have wanted to gather your children together as a hen protects her chicks beneath her wings, but you wouldn't let me."** *Matthew 23:37*

Jesus dies on the cross for everyone, including those who rejected Him. He suffers for His brothers, His hometown, Gentiles, Samaritans, the religious leaders who arrested Him and the soldiers who nailed Him to the cross.

As followers of Jesus, we should not be surprised when people reject us, even when we are doing good to them.

> **"If the world hates you, remember that it hated me first."** *John 15:18*

When hated and rejected, we react as Jesus did.

> **Don't repay evil for evil. Don't retaliate with insults when people insult you. Instead, pay them back with a**

blessing. That is what God has called you to do, and he will grant you his blessing. *1 Peter 3:9*

For Reflection

1. Recall a time when you did something good for someone and they turned against you. How did that make you feel?

2. Why do you think many people today reject Jesus?

3. Why didn't rejection discourage Jesus from His mission?

Living the Messiah

1. Pray for someone who has rejected your attempts to bless them.

2. Find a way to help someone who has rejected you, preferably without their knowing the help came from you.

Prayer

Despised and rejected One, thank you for being faithful to your calling and for dying for us, even when we rejected you. May we never be ashamed of you!

DAY FIFTEEN:
WOUNDED

Surely He hath borne our griefs, and carried our sorrows. He was wounded for our transgressions, He was bruised for our iniquities, the chastisement of our peace was upon Him. And with His stripes we are healed. *Isaiah 53:4–5*

Some call Isaiah 53 "the Fifth Gospel" because it so clearly describes the suffering of Jesus.

The Holy Spirit sends the disciple Phillip to the road from Jerusalem to Gaza where he meets with the treasurer of Ethiopia who is traveling in a chariot along the road. The Spirit tells Phillip to walk beside the chariot. Phillip hears the man reading the Bible and asks him if he understands what he is reading. The man invites him into his chariot where he had been reading Isaiah 53:7-8. The Ethiopian then asks an important question:

And the eunuch said to Philip, "About whom, I ask you, does the prophet say this, about himself or about someone else?" Then Philip opened his mouth, and beginning with this Scripture he told him the good news

about Jesus. And as they were going along the road they came to some water, and the eunuch said, "See, here is water! What prevents me from being baptized?" And he commanded the chariot to stop, and they both went down into the water, Philip and the eunuch, and he baptized him. *Acts 8:34-38 (ESV)*

The Meaning in Isaiah

Do these words apply to Jesus and not to anyone in Isaiah's time? Or (as we saw earlier) could it be that there is a near meaning in the day of the prophet and a far meaning in the life of the Messiah to come?

To whom could these words refer in Isaiah's day?

Some think they are a poetic and hyperbolic way to describe the experience of Isaiah himself. This was the first thought of the Ethiopian, that the prophet is talking of himself. If so, Isaiah is speaking of himself in the third person, "he." Or in this part of Isaiah, it is the followers of the prophet who are speaking about him. This would be another passage in the writings of the prophets where they lament their calling yet embrace suffering for the sake of the nation.

Others think the Suffering Servant is Israel. "He" in these verses would be a collective noun for the nation. God is telling Israel that they all will suffer in exile. Yet this chapter ends with a promise of restoration, hope, and glory for Isaiah the prophet and for Israel.

> But it was the Lord's good plan to crush him
> and cause him grief.
> Yet when his life is made an offering for sin,
> he will have many descendants.
> He will enjoy a long life,
> and the Lord's good plan will prosper in his hands.
> When he sees all that is accomplished by his anguish,
> and he will be satisfied.
> And because of his experience,

> my righteous servant will make it possible
> for many to be counted righteous,
> for he will bear all their sins.
> I will give him the honors of a victorious soldier,
> because he exposed himself to death.
> He was counted among the rebels.
> He bore the sins of many and interceded for rebels.
> *Isaiah 53:10-12*

The Meaning in Jesus

These words about the Suffering Servant in Isaiah so obviously point to Jesus, that it is hard to hear them another way. It is surprising, then, to learn that most students of the Bible in the time of Jesus did not apply these words to the Messiah who was to come. From other Bible passages they correctly expected the Messiah to be a conquering king who freed them from their enemies and established a just kingdom in Israel. They did not expect a defeated, shamed, and executed Messiah.

This lack of the fuller understanding of Isaiah 53 explains why even the apostles could not fathom a dying Messiah. When Jesus asks them who he is, Peter rightly says, "You are the Messiah" (Matthew 16:16). Jesus blesses Peter for that great confession,. but when Jesus immediately begins to speak of His suffering and dying, Peter takes Him aside to correct Him.

> But Peter took him aside and began to reprimand him for saying such things. "Heaven forbid, Lord," he said. "This will never happen to you!"
> Jesus turned to Peter and said, "Get away from me, Satan! You are a dangerous trap to me. You are seeing things merely from a human point of view, not from God's." *Matthew 16:22-23*

Peter has the prevailing view of his time—that the Messiah will conquer and reign—but it is a faulty human perspective. God intends the Messiah to conquer and rule through sacrificial suffering. Jesus is the be the ultimate Suffering Servant as described in Isaiah.

This faulty view—that Jesus can go to glory without first going to the cross—shows up in the story of the temptation of Jesus. Satan tempts Jesus to provide for His every desire by turning stones to bread. He tempts Him to test that God will keep Him from all harm by jumping off the temple so angels will protect Him. He tempts Jesus to rule the world without experiencing suffering and death (Matthew 4:1-11, Luke 4:1-13). But Jesus knows that the way to glory always goes through the cross.

The idea that a dead man cannot be the true Messiah also appears in the story of the two disciples on the road to Emmaus. Their hope that Jesus was the one who would save Israel is dashed by His crucifixion. When the risen Jesus appears to them on the road (but they do not recognize Him), He gives them a fuller understanding of the Bible.

> **Then Jesus said to them, "You foolish people! You find it so hard to believe all that the prophets wrote in the Scriptures. Wasn't it clearly predicted that the Messiah would have to suffer all these things before entering his glory?" Then Jesus took them through the writings of Moses and all the prophets, explaining from all the Scriptures the things concerning himself.**
> *Luke 24:25-27*

I've got to believe that one of the prophetic writings Jesus took them through is Isaiah 53. Yet they do not recognize Jesus in the Bible lesson. They only see Him when He breaks bread with them.

In the same way, it is when we (by faith) see the resurrected Jesus that we more fully understand the description of Him as the Suffering Messiah in Isaiah and other Bible passages.

Meaning for Us

This discussion of the near and far meanings of the words of Isaiah should not distract us from the power of their meaning for us. Read again these words from Isaiah out loud, and emphasize the following words—"our" and "we."

> **Surely He hath borne our griefs, and carried our sorrows. He was wounded for our transgressions, He was bruised for our iniquities, the chastisement of our peace was upon Him. And with His stripes we are healed.** *Isaiah 53:4-5*

Jesus is the Lamb of God who takes away the sins of the world. How? By being a sacrifice for us. By being the ransom for us. And in this passage, by taking our place. We deserved suffering. He took it for us,

We might react to that with guilt and shame. It was our sins that put Him on the cross, but the stress in these verses is not on our transgressions and iniquities, it is on what Jesus as the Suffering Servant has done for us. Read it out loud, one more time, with special attention on these words—"borne," "carried," "peace" and "healed." These are the gifts of the Messiah

For Reflection

1. Does it diminish the power of these words if they can apply to Isaiah or Israel as well as to Jesus? Why or why not?

2. Why would some not want a Messiah who suffers and dies?

3. How does suffering lead to glory?

Living the Messiah

1. Take the time to slowly read all of Isaiah 53 out loud, then meditate on it.

2. Find a way to suffer for someone else. Do that with trust
   and joy.

Prayer

Jesus who suffered for us, we thank you for all that suffering
accomplished. Father who rewarded the suffering of Jesus with life
and glory, help us as we suffer for others.

DAY SIXTEEN:
ASTRAY

All we like sheep have gone astray; we have turned everyone to his own way, and the Lord hath laid on Him the iniquity of us all. *Isaiah 53:6*

We have already seen *Messiah* picture the Lord as a Shepherd and His people as sheep. Now we turn back to two characteristics of sheep; they frequently get lost and are easily led.

Led Astray

The Bible begins with the story of a God who creates a beautiful garden for humans to live in and care for. God has an intimate relationship with man and woman in the garden, walking and talking with them. Everything is the way God intends.

That is, until a serpent appears and leads the woman and the man to go astray from the path to life God had planned for them. Why would they leave the Source of life itself? Because the serpent promises that they will "be like God, knowing both good and evil" (Genesis 3:5).

Did Eve and Adam not know what was evil? Had God not told them not to eat of the fruit of that particular tree? They already knew it was wrong to eat it. "Know" here means to experience. They had only experienced good before they ate the fruit. Now they experience evil, having been fooled into thinking that evil was better for them. They already were like God, made in His image (Genesis 1:27). The serpent fooled them into thinking they could be their own gods, ruling their lives and making their decisions based on what looked good and tasted good to them.

Adam and Eve seem amazingly naïve, and history has shown their descendants to also be easily led. Humans tend to follow whoever promises them a better life, instead of following the Author and Source of life. Some deceive them into following other "gods," trusting that they will give assured blessings—crops, health, power, and peace. God warns His people against following those who will lead them to wander into the path of death.

> **Serve only the Lord your God and fear him alone. Obey his commands, listen to his voice, and cling to him. The false prophets or visionaries who try to lead you astray must be put to death, for they encourage rebellion against the Lord your God, who redeemed you from slavery and brought you out of the land of Egypt. Since they try to lead you astray from the way the Lord your God commanded you to live, you must put them to death. In this way you will purge the evil from among you.**
> *Deuteronomy 13:4-5*

Capital punishment for false prophets seems harsh to us. Shouldn't they be allowed their freedom of speech? But they are separating God's people from the one who gives life. By leading people to their deaths, they are no better than murderers.

Sometimes, even those who are to guide God's people lead them astray.

> "My people have been lost sheep.
> Their shepherds have led them astray
> and turned them loose in the mountains.
> They have lost their way
> and can't remember how to get back to the sheepfold."
> *Jeremiah 50:6*

When following human leaders we must always ask, are they leading us to the Good Shepherd or have they turned us loose to get lost in the mountains of confusion, doubt, and danger?

Drifting

Sometimes others lead us astray. At other times, we do not need someone to lead us into danger. We drift into it by ourselves.

So the Psalmist prays:

> **Don't let me drift toward evil**
> **or take part in acts of wickedness.**
> **Don't let me share in the delicacies**
> **of those who do wrong.** *Psalm 141:4*

It takes no effort to drift away from the Lord. We just do less. We neglect our prayer time each day. We skip our Bible reading. We give up the habit of meeting with other Christians. We sleepwalk through our days without awareness of the presence of God. With physical exercise, if you keep postponing your workout, you might not notice a difference for a while. But eventually it catches up to you. In the same way, we often do not realize we have drifted from God until it is too late. We need a strong warning.

> **So we must listen very carefully to the truth we have**
> **heard, or we may drift away from it. For the message God**
> **delivered through angels has always stood firm, and**
> **every violation of the law and every act of disobedience**
> **was punished. So what makes us think we can escape if**

we ignore this great salvation that was first announced by the Lord Jesus himself and then delivered to us by those who heard him speak? *Hebrews 2:1-3*

One sign of that drifting is that we begin to lose confidence in our salvation. We forget the good news that Jesus saves us by His grace.

Yet now he has reconciled you to himself through the death of Christ in his physical body. As a result, he has brought you into his own presence, and you are holy and blameless as you stand before him without a single fault. But you must continue to believe this truth and stand firmly in it. Don't drift away from the assurance you received when you heard the Good News. *Colossians 1:22-23*

In light of our tendency to wander and drift, it is hard to believe we are holy, blameless, and without fault. That's why we need to be consistent in our prayer, Bible study, fellowship, worship, and service. These regular practices do not make us faultless; they remind us that we have right relationship with God through Christ.

Wander

Sheep wander here and there with no sense of direction. They need to be penned in to be saved.

God's people are also prone to wander. Out of concern for them, the Lord gave them His law, His instruction, to guide them and keep them safe. Psalm 119 (the longest Psalm) is praise for that law. It seems strange to us to praise because it restricts our freedom. Don't tread on me! But the law of God protects His people from wandering into danger.

I used to wander off until you disciplined me; but now I closely follow your word. *Psalm 119:67*

> **I have wandered away like a lost sheep; come and find me, for I have not forgotten your commands.** *Psalm 119:176*

The great news is that when God's people wander away from Him, He pursues them and brings them back. Even when the Lord sent them into exile, He promised to embrace them again.

> **How long will you wander,**
> **my wayward daughter?**
> **For the Lord will cause something new to happen—**
> **Israel will embrace her God.**
> **This is what the Lord of Heaven's Armies, the God of Israel, says: "When I bring them back from captivity, the people of Judah and its towns will again say,**
> **'The Lord bless you, O righteous home, O holy mountain!'"** *Jeremiah 31:22-23*

We have been led astray. We have drifted. We wandered. But God has brought us back to His fold. He restores the relationship He desired with humanity from the beginning. He has done this through Jesus, the Messiah, the Great Shepherd.

> **He personally carried our sins**
> **in his body on the cross**
> **so that we can be dead to sin**
> **and live for what is right.**
> **By his wounds**
> **you are healed.**
> **Once you were like sheep**
> **who wandered away.**
> **But now you have turned to your Shepherd,**
> **the Guardian of your souls.** *1 Peter 2:24-25*

Having returned to our Shepherd, we have the responsibility to lead others to return to Him.

My dear brothers and sisters, if someone among you wanders away from the truth and is brought back, you can be sure that whoever brings the sinner back from wandering will save that person from death and bring about the forgiveness of many sins. *James 5:19-20*

We have strayed like sheep. That is not good news. The Lamb of God gave Himself to bring us to God. That's the best news of all.

For Reflection

1. What is more likely, that you will deliberately turn against God, or that you will drift away from Him? Why?

2. What are some ways we can support and trust our spiritual leaders and, at the same time, guard against being led astray?

3. What should we do to keep from drifting and wandering?

Living the Messiah

1. Identify something specific that leads you away from Jesus—money, alcohol, your need for approval, or something else. Ask Jesus through the Spirit to give you the power to see through the deception and resist.

2. Encourage someone who is drifting away from relationship with Jesus.

Prayer

Lord, we are so easily distracted and led into paths of death. Open our eyes so we may see your hand guiding us with love.

DAY SEVENTEEN:
SCORN

All they that see Him, laugh Him to scorn; they shoot out their lips, and shake their heads, saying: He trusted in God that He would deliver Him; let Him deliver Him, if He delight in Him *Psalm 22:7-8*

I've always thought I had a good sense of humor. I particularly am able to make fun of myself. Self-deprecating humor is usually a sign of a healthy ego. We all have close friends who can put us down with a smile without hurting our feelings.

I confess that I've used humor to taunt others. Perhaps you have done the same. Why do we belittle others? Perhaps we do it to make ourselves look clever, meaning no harm. Or do we do it deliberately to make ourselves look better than others? Often we do it to harm. Whoever said, "sticks and stones may break my bones, but words will never hurt me," had no idea what they were saying. Yes, physical violence may hurt more at first, but the wounds from hateful words last longer.

I can laugh at myself, but I do not want you to laugh at me, particularly when I am in pain.

Scorned Psalmist

These words from *Messiah* come from Psalm 22, one of the best known laments in the Bible. The opening words to the Psalm are familiar.

> **My God, my God, why have you forsaken me?**
> **Why are you so far from saving me, from the words of**
> **my groaning?**
> **O my God, I cry by day, but you do not answer,**
> **and by night, but I find no rest.** *Psalm 22:1-2 (ESV)*

Does the Psalmist really feel completely abandoned by God? Does he feel that God will not answer his prayers? Certainly he does. David, traditionally the writer of this Psalm, must have felt this way often when he was running away from Saul and when it looked like everyone was against him.

Have you ever felt this way? Abandoned by God? Thinking God is ignoring your cries? I've known well-meaning Christians who hear sentiments like this from their fellow believers and tell them, "You shouldn't feel that way." They see these honest screams to God as signs of unbelief.

I've never found it helpful to be told to ignore my uncontrollable feelings. It's never good to deny how we feel. What's more, the Bible has many such heart-felt cries of abandonment. They are not signs of despair, but are faithful laments to God.

What makes them faithful laments? First of all, they are spoken to the Lord. The Psalmist is not complaining about God to others, he is talking to the One who has disappointed him. "Lord, you're not listening to my prayer" is itself a prayer! When you feel abandoned by God, tell Him! He can take it. When everyone makes fun of you because of your faith, tell the Lord about it. Being candid with God is not doubt, it is holding on to the precious relationship we have with Him.

Biblical laments are also faithful laments. Although they begin with plain-spoken grievances with God, they end with confidence that God will hear, act, and save. That's the way this psalm ends.

> **I will proclaim your name to my brothers and sisters.**
> **I will praise you among your assembled people.**
> **Praise the Lord, all you who fear him!**
> **Honor him, all you descendants of Jacob!**
> **Show him reverence, all you descendants of Israel!**
> **For he has not ignored or belittled the suffering of the needy.**
> **He has not turned his back on them,**
> **but has listened to their cries for help.** *Psalm 22:22-24*

The Psalmist feels forsaken by God, but he is not forsaken! Deep down the Psalmist trusts that God will never turn His back on him. Others may belittle us, but the Lord will not belittle our suffering.

Scorned Jesus

Jesus knew what it was like to be scorned, mocked, and ridiculed. At his trial, when Pilate hears that Jesus is from Galilee he sends Him to Herod Antipas for judgment. Herod finds Jesus innocent, but still wants to have some fun at His expense.

> **Then Herod and his soldiers began mocking and ridiculing Jesus. Finally, they put a royal robe on him and sent him back to Pilate.** *Luke 23:11*

Presumably, these soldiers were Jews. Why would Jews belittle Jesus since He was also a Jew? These soldiers had cast their lot with Herod Antipas, a client king of Rome. Since Herod was their king, they humiliate Jesus as a pretend king, putting a royal robe on Him.

How does Jesus react to this attempt to disgrace Him? He suffers in silence, refusing to answer Herod's questions (Luke 23:9).

Pilate's soldiers also taunted Jesus.

> **Some of the governor's soldiers took Jesus into their headquarters and called out the entire regiment. They stripped him and put a scarlet robe on him. They wove thorn branches into a crown and put it on his head, and they placed a reed stick in his right hand as a scepter. Then they knelt before him in mockery and taunted, "Hail! King of the Jews!" And they spit on him and grabbed the stick and struck him on the head with it. When they were finally tired of mocking him, they took off the robe and put his own clothes on him again. Then they led him away to be crucified.** *Matthew 27:27-31*

Here the mockery is physical as well as verbal—they hit Him on the crown of thorns and spit on Him, in addition to ridiculing Him as a pretend king. These Roman soldiers may be taking out their frustrations on all Jews by degrading Jesus.

The hatred of soldiers at a rival king may be understandable but not excusable. Harder to understand is the deep anger that many of the Jewish religious leaders showed toward Jesus. Not content to see Him crucified, they add insult to injury.

> **The leading priests, the teachers of religious law, and the elders also mocked Jesus. "He saved others," they scoffed, "but he can't save himself! So he is the King of Israel, is he? Let him come down from the cross right now, and we will believe in him! He trusted God, so let God rescue him now if he wants him! For he said, 'I am the Son of God.'"** *Matthew 27:41-43*

When Jesus heard these words, He must have thought of Psalm 22:7-8. How does He react to the shame heaped upon Him by the soldiers and the religious leaders? Does He curse them back? Does He call angels to destroy them? No. He says, "Father, forgive them, for they don't know what they are doing" (Luke 23:34). He dies for the sins of those who shame Him.

What's more, He trusts God to save Him. Jesus certainly feels forsaken on the cross, but He is not forsaken. Like the Psalmist, He trusts that God will deliver Him. And God does that powerfully in the resurrection.

Facing Scorn

It may be hard for us to imagine being surrounded by enemies like David was when he wrote Psalm 22. It's even harder to relate to being mocked, beaten, spat upon, crucified, and jeered.

But we also face put downs as Christians. "She thinks she's better than anyone else." "There he goes, he hates gays and liberals and everyone else." "At least I'm not a hypocrite like those Christians."

These are some of the milder things we sometimes hear if we have faith in Jesus. How do we react?

Jesus not only shows us how to react to scorn and mocking, but He also tells us it is a blessing!

> **God blesses you when people mock you and persecute you and lie about you and say all sorts of evil things against you because you are my followers. Be happy about it! Be very glad! For a great reward awaits you in heaven. And remember, the ancient prophets were persecuted in the same way.** *Matthew 5:11-12*

We Christians sometimes deserve ridicule. We need to act more like Jesus did and show love to all our neighbors. No one likes to be made fun of, and we are called not to enjoy the scorn, but to trust the God who delivered the Psalmist, the prophets, and Jesus.

For Reflection

1. Have you ever felt forsaken by God? How did you react?

2. How should we treat those who ridicule us as Christians?

3. Why is it so hard to trust in God when others are making fun of us?

Living the Messiah

1. Pray for those who belittle you for acting like a Christian.

2. Live in such a way that the criticism you receive because you are a Christian is never justified.

Prayer

Jesus who was mocked and spat upon, hear our cries when those around us scorn us and harm us. Give us the faith to be bold in our witness especially when we face mocking.

DAY EIGHTEEN:
SORROW

Thy rebuke hath broken His heart; He is full of heaviness; He looked for some to have pity on Him, but there was no man, neither found He any to comfort Him. *Psalm 69:20*

Behold, and see if there be any sorrow like unto His sorrow. *Lamentations 1:12*

Somewhere along the line, American Christianity became overwhelmed with positive thinking. Many Christians believe they should be happy and cheerful all day long in order to be genuine followers of Jesus.

What's wrong with positive thinking? Shouldn't Christians be optimistic?

A superficial optimism is shallow, and does not help those who truly grieve. Using Bible verses to focus on the sunny side of life usually takes those verses out of their biblical context and makes them into magical mantras. True biblical faith, based on hope, not optimism, embraces all of life—sorrow as well as joy.

Israel and Sorrow

As we have seen, those who trust the Lord in the Old Testament keep their hope in Him during their darkest times. They lament in trust. The words above from *Messiah* are from another lament in Psalms that begins

> **Save me, O God,**
> **for the floodwaters are up to my neck.**
> **Deeper and deeper I sink into the mire;**
> **I can't find a foothold.**
> **I am in deep water,**
> **and the floods overwhelm me.**
> **I am exhausted from crying for help;**
> **my throat is parched.**
> **My eyes are swollen with weeping,**
> **waiting for my God to help me.** *Psalm 69:1-3*

If you've ever felt like you were drowning in your difficulties, you can relate to this Psalm. If you've ever cried your eyes out, you know how the Psalmist feels. In those times it seems that there is no one who comforts us, only those who break our hearts.

> **Their insults have broken my heart,**
> **and I am in despair.**
> **If only one person would show some pity;**
> **if only one would turn and comfort me.** *Psalm 69:20*

Note that there is no positive thinking here, only an honest, heart-felt cry to God. This overwhelming sorrow is not only personal, but it is wailing for all of God's people. The book of Lamentations begins with those tears:

> Jerusalem, once so full of people,
> is now deserted.
> She who was once great among the nations
> now sits alone like a widow.
> Once the queen of all the earth,
> she is now a slave.
> She sobs through the night;
> tears stream down her cheeks.
> Among all her lovers,
> there is no one left to comfort her.
> All her friends have betrayed her
> and become her enemies. *Lamentations 1:1-2*

God's people have turned against Him and He has sent them into exile. Jerusalem is destroyed. No wonder the writer of Lamentations feels that there is no sorrow like this.

Jesus and Sorrow

But surely God sent Jesus to earth to take away our sorrow. Yes, but He takes it away, not by ignoring it through sunny-side thinking, but by completely sharing in human sorrow. We have no passages in the Bible that speak of Jesus putting on a happy face or telling people that things were not so bad. We do have stories of His crying bitterly in sorrow. When He sees Mary and others weeping at the tomb of Lazarus, He shares their pain.

> When Jesus saw her weeping and saw the other people wailing with her, a deep anger welled up within him, and he was deeply troubled. "Where have you put him?" he asked them.
> They told him, "Lord, come and see." Then Jesus wept. The people who were standing nearby said, "See how much he loved him!" *John 11:33-36*

That Jesus wept here has always puzzled me. He knew he was about to raise Lazarus from the dead, so why would He cry over him? He cries when He sees others crying. He shares their grief and pain. I also wonder if He is deeply moved, even angered, by death itself. Death was not God's plan from the beginning. Jesus may be crying not just in the face of the death of Lazarus, but also in light of all the deaths that humans ever will experience. The pain of separation at death is real, but it is not final. In the end, death will be no more and God will wipe away all tears (Revelation 21:4). The resurrection of Lazarus prefigures the resurrection of all.

The heart of Jesus is also broken by the unbelief of His people.

> **But as he came closer to Jerusalem and saw the city ahead, he began to weep. "How I wish today that you of all people would understand the way to peace. But now it is too late, and peace is hidden from your eyes. Before long your enemies will build ramparts against your walls and encircle you and close in on you from every side. They will crush you into the ground, and your children with you. Your enemies will not leave a single stone in place, because you did not recognize it when God visited you."** *Luke 19:41-44*

As in the Book of Lamentations, Jesus grieves and cries over the destruction of Jerusalem. Like the Father, Jesus never rejoices when He has to discipline His people. He does everything to bring them back to Him. If you have ever had your heart broken by the choices of your children, you know how this feels.

Jesus also knows what it is like to feel that God has abandoned Him. He prays His most heartfelt prayer in the Garden of Gethsemane, "Father, let this cup of suffering pass." This also was a faithful lament because He prayed, "Yet I want your will to be done, not mine" (Matthew 26:39). Tears accompanied this ardent prayer.

> **While Jesus was here on earth, he offered prayers and pleadings, with a loud cry and tears, to the one who could rescue him from death. And God heard his prayers because of his deep reverence for God.** *Hebrews 5:7*

Jesus sufferers for us. He entrusts His suffering to God and God hears His prayer. The Father does not remove the suffering on the cross, but He saves Jesus through resurrection.

Our Suffering

What does this mean for followers of Jesus?

First, it means that Jesus suffers for us and with us. He cries with us when we lose those we love, just as He wept at the tomb of Lazarus. He understands when we feel forsaken, because He felt that way Himself. He shares our pain because He suffered on the cross.

Jesus gives meaning to our suffering.

> **Not only that, but we rejoice in our sufferings, knowing that suffering produces endurance, and endurance produces character, and character produces hope, and hope does not put us to shame, because God's love has been poured into our hearts through the Holy Spirit who has been given to us.** *Romans 5:3-5 (ESV)*

And no matter how severe our suffering, Jesus promises an end to suffering and give us an eternal weight of glory.

> **Yet what we suffer now is nothing compared to the glory he will reveal to us later.** *Romans 8:18*

Since Jesus shares our sorrows, He calls us to "weep with those who weep" (Romans 12:15).

For Reflection

1. What's wrong with positive thinking? Are there times we should look on the bright side? Are there times when positive thinking is harmful?

2. Did Jesus suffer disappointment, heartbreak, and pain just like we do? Or was it easier for him as the Son of God?

3. What are some ways we can share in the sorrows of others?

Living the Messiah

1. Take your suffering to God in prayer through Jesus, trusting that He understands and that God will act.

2. Find a way to help someone who is suffering.

Prayer

Suffering Jesus, shed your tears for us this day. Be with us in our rejection and pain. Increase our trust in God to save us.

DAY NINETEEN:
DEATH

He was cut off out of the land of the living: for the transgression of Thy people was He stricken. *Isaiah 53:8*

But Thou didst not leave His soul in hell, nor didst Thou suffer Thy Holy One to see corruption. *Psalm 16:10*

"Where did Jesus go when He died?" asked a young girl in our church.

It sounds like an easy question to answer, but it is not.

Sheol

The Hebrew word translated "hell" in Psalm 16:10, is *sheol*. In the Hebrew Bible the word does not refer to hell as we think of it, but to the place of the dead. The Hebrews thought that the dead go to the grave, sheol, a place under the earth, a "dark pit" (Psalm 88:6, 11-12). Those in sheol can no longer give praise to God (Psalm 6:5, Isaiah 38:18), yet the Lord's presence is even in sheol (Psalm 139:7-8).

Job laments that one cannot return to life from sheol (Job 7:9, 10:21, 16:22). When David learns his child is dead, he says

"But why should I fast when he is dead? Can I bring him back again? I will go to him one day, but he cannot return to me." *2 Samuel 12:23*

There is the story of Saul disguising himself and asking a medium to call the spirit of Samuel back from the dead. When she does so, she describes what she sees as a god coming up out of the earth and an old man in a robe (see 1 Samuel 28:3-25). We might think this story would give Israel hope of life after death, but in fact the law and prophets expressly condemned the practice of calling up spirits (Leviticus 19:31; Deuteronomy 18:10–12; Isaiah 8:19).

Not only is sheol a place of darkness, but the descriptions of it in the Old Testament are dark and vague. In Old Testament times, it seems that God did not give his people a clear picture of the afterlife. By the time of Jesus, there were two schools of thought. The Sadducees believed one never returned from sheol, while the Pharisees came to believe in resurrection.

So where did the spirit of Jesus go when He died? Between His crucifixion and resurrection, He went to sheol, the place of the dead.

Now that he ascended, what is it but that he also descended first into the lower parts of the earth? *Ephesians 4:9 (KJV)*

Hell

A theological tradition called the "harrowing of hell" states that between the crucifixion and resurrection Jesus went to hell and saved some who were there. One passage in the New Testament might point in this direction.

For Christ also suffered once for sins, the righteous for the unrighteous, that he might bring us to God, being put to death in the flesh but made alive in the spirit, in which he went and proclaimed to the spirits in prison, because

they formerly did not obey, when God's patience waited in the days of Noah, while the ark was being prepared, in which a few, that is, eight persons, were brought safely through water. *1 Peter 3:18-20 (ESV)*

These are some of the hardest verses to understand in the New Testament. Scholars have written hundreds of pages on this passage. Here is an extremely brief summary of the three traditional interpretations.

1. Jesus was alive through the Holy Spirit in the person of Noah, who warned the people of his day about the coming flood. In this view, these verses say nothing about where the spirit of Jesus was between the crucifixion and the resurrection.
2. After the crucifixion, the spirit of Jesus went to hell and proclaimed the just punishment of those who disobeyed in the time of Noah.
3. As a spirit after His death, Jesus went into hell and preached the good news of His sacrifice for all sin, giving those disobedient in Noah's day (and perhaps all who lived before the death of Jesus) an opportunity for repentance.

Some think the following verse also points to Jesus preaching the gospel to the dead.

For this is why the gospel was preached even to those who are dead, that though judged in the flesh the way people are, they might live in the spirit the way God does. *1 Peter 4:6*

After studying these passages from Peter for years, I'm still not sure what they mean. But many Christians confess that Jesus descended into hell and brought hope to those who were dead.

Paradise

After He died, Jesus went to be with his Father in Paradise. That's what I told the little girl at church. That's where Jesus said He was going when He spoke to the penitent on the cross next to His.

> **One of the criminals who were hanged railed at him, saying, "Are you not the Christ? Save yourself and us!" But the other rebuked him, saying, "Do you not fear God, since you are under the same sentence of condemnation? And we indeed justly, for we are receiving the due reward of our deeds; but this man has done nothing wrong." And he said, "Jesus, remember me when you come into your kingdom." And he said to him, "Truly, I say to you, today you will be with me in paradise."** *Luke 23:39-43 (ESV)*

What is paradise? The Greek word means a beautiful garden. Paul uses the word to describe a vision or a bodily experience he had.

> **I was caught up to the third heaven fourteen years ago. Whether I was in my body or out of my body, I don't know—only God knows. Yes, only God knows whether I was in my body or outside my body. But I do know that I was caught up to paradise and heard things so astounding that they cannot be expressed in words, things no human is allowed to tell.** *2 Corinthians 12:2-4*

Paul equates paradise with the "third heaven." The first heaven is the sky, the second is where the stars reside, and the third is where God lives. Therefore, Jesus promises the thief on the cross that he will be with Jesus in the presence of God immediately after death.

So where did Jesus go between his death and resurrection—sheol, hell, or paradise? Perhaps all three. While His body was in the tomb, His spirit went to sheol—the place of the dead. He was in the section of sheol called paradise, where the righteous go, but He also proclaimed salvation to those already dead.

This detour into where Jesus went after death should not lead us away from the amazing truth in the words from *Messiah*. Isaiah 53:8 says the Suffering Servant "was cut off out of the land of the living." Applied to Jesus, they show that He was truly dead. He experienced death as all humans do.

The great news, as we will see later in *Messiah*, is that God did not leave the spirit of Jesus in sheol, did not "leave his soul in hell" (Psalm 16:10) but united the spirit or soul of Jesus with a resurrected body.

The ultimate paradise will be in the new heaven and earth.

> **Anyone with ears to hear must listen to the Spirit and understand what he is saying to the churches. To everyone who is victorious I will give fruit from the tree of life in the paradise of God.** *Revelation 2:7*

In the original paradise of Eden, the Lord planted the tree of life to sustain humanity (Genesis 2:9). Death was not in God's original plan. The Lord will renew and enhance that paradise in the new heavens and earth.

> **Then the angel showed me a river with the water of life, clear as crystal, flowing from the throne of God and of the Lamb. It flowed down the center of the main street. On each side of the river grew a tree of life, bearing twelve crops of fruit, with a fresh crop each month. The leaves were used for medicine to heal the nations.**
> **No longer will there be a curse upon anything. For the throne of God and of the Lamb will be there, and his servants will worship him. And they will see his face, and his name will be written on their foreheads. And there will be no night there—no need for lamps or sun—for the**

Lord God will shine on them. And they will reign forever and ever. *Revelation 22:1-5*

May the day come quickly when we join with Jesus the Messiah, the Lamb, in paradise.

For Reflection

1. Why didn't God give those in Old Testament times as clear a portrait of the afterlife than what He gave later?

2. Has God given us a complete picture of what happens after death?

3. Why is it important that Jesus suffered the same kind of death and afterlife as everyone?

Living the Messiah

1. Take some time to think about your own death. See how that changes how you live today.

2. Without denying the reality of death, comfort someone who has lost a loved one. .

Prayer

Lord God, as you did not leave Jesus in the place of the dead, so raise us up through the power of the Spirit. May we trust you as Jesus trusted that he would be with you after death.

DAY TWENTY:
GLORY

Lift up your heads, O ye gates, and be ye lift up, ye everlasting doors, and the King of Glory shall come in. Who is this King of Glory? The Lord strong and mighty, the Lord mighty in battle. Lift up your heads, O ye gates; and be ye lift up, ye everlasting doors; and the King of Glory shall come in. Who is this King of Glory? The Lord of Hosts, He is the King of Glory. *Psalm 24:7–10*

There's nothing more exciting to a sports fan than to see their favorite team snatch victory from defeat. In baseball, it's the thrill of the walk-off homer. Basketball fans have the buzzer-beater. While time expires, the "hail mary" pass for a winning touchdown is the joy of football. What is so wonderful about these moments is that they come when you had resigned yourself to a heart-breaking loss.

In the same way, Handel's *Messiah* traces the story of Jesus to the cross, the most profound experience of shame and defeat. Evil has triumphed over good. Satan has conquered the Messiah. Hope has died.

But wait. This is not the end of the story. What looks like the ultimate defeat is actually the path to glory.

The Glory of the Creator

Psalm 24 begins with recognizing the glory of God in creation.

> **The earth is the Lord's, and everything in it.**
> **The world and all its people belong to him.**
> **For he laid the earth's foundation on the seas**
> **and built it on the ocean depths.** *Psalm 24:1-2*

Many scholars think this psalm celebrates bringing the Ark of the Covenant into the temple. If so, it begins with the reminder that the entire creation is God's home, not just a building in Jerusalem. We serve a big God! He is beyond our imagination. No building or tribe or country can contain Him. When we look at the beauty and scope of His creation, we catch a glimpse of His glory. More than that, we want to become part of that majestic glory. We long for a relationship with the loving Creator.

Seeking Glory

How do we enter into the glorious presence of God? What must we do to seek relationship with Him?

> **Who may climb the mountain of the Lord?**
> **Who may stand in his holy place?**
> **Only those whose hands and hearts are pure,**
> **who do not worship idols**
> **and never tell lies.**
> **They will receive the Lord's blessing**
> **and have a right relationship with God their savior.**
> **Such people may seek you**
> **and worship in your presence, O God of Jacob.**
> *Psalm 24:3-6*

Relationship with God is a gift, but it is a gift we must seek. This is not works righteousness but an expression of genuine trust in the Lord. We must seek Him sincerely. We must worship Him alone. We must speak and live the truth. Then the Lord will bless us with His presence. We dare not rush into the glory of God, demanding our rights. We enter humbly and wholeheartedly, knowing that we approach the Creator of all things.

Triumphal Glory

We can enter into the life of God, His glory, only because He first entered our lives.

> **Open up, ancient gates!**
> **Open up, ancient doors,**
> **and let the King of glory enter.**
> **Who is the King of glory?**
> **The Lord, strong and mighty;**
> **the Lord, invincible in battle.**
> **Open up, ancient gates!**
> **Open up, ancient doors,**
> **and let the King of glory enter.**
> **Who is the King of glory?**
> **The Lord of Heaven's Armies—**
> **he is the King of glory.** *Psalm 24:7-10*

The one who enters the temple of our lives is the conquering King. He is the Almighty Lord who fights for us and defeats our enemies. No power can stand before Him.

Jesus the Creator

And how does that King of Glory come triumphantly into us as His temple? He becomes flesh in Jesus of Nazareth. He comes as a King in a manger, not a palace. He comes as one poor, not rich. He dies the lowest death, as a criminal on the cross. Yet this one who dies is the King of Glory. What we say about the Father we can also say of Him.

117

With the Father, Jesus is the Creator of all things.

> **God created everything through him, and nothing was created except through him.** *John 1:3*

> **Christ is the visible image of the invisible God.**
> **He existed before anything was created and is supreme over all creation, for through him God created everything in the heavenly realms and on earth.** *Colossians 1:16-17*

This is a great mystery of our faith, to believe that the Creator of all things died on a cross on Calvary. To say that God is dead is to admit absolute defeat, but through the death of the Creator comes the creation of a new heaven and earth.

Seeking the Glory

How do we share in the glory of Jesus? How do we enter the presence of God through Him? Through purity of heart (Matthew 5:18). In the words of Søren Kierkegaard (1813-1855), "purity of heart is to will one thing." The one thing we desire is to be in the presence of the Holy God through the work of Jesus. That's what Jesus gives us, entry into the glorious presence!

> **This High Priest of ours understands our weaknesses, for he faced all of the same testings we do, yet he did not sin. So let us come boldly to the throne of our gracious God. There we will receive his mercy, and we will find grace to help us when we need it most.** *Hebrews 4:15-16*

The death of Jesus on the cross is not a defeat but a victory! By giving Himself for us, He became the great High Priest who opens the doors so the King of Glory can enter our hearts as His temple.

Triumphal Glory

As the Lord fought the battles of his people Israel and triumphed over their enemies, so Jesus on the cross defeats the greatest enemies of all.

You were dead because of your sins and because your sinful nature was not yet cut away. Then God made you alive with Christ, for he forgave all our sins. He canceled the record of the charges against us and took it away by nailing it to the cross. In this way, he disarmed the spiritual rulers and authorities. He shamed them publicly by his victory over them on the cross. *Colossians 2:13-15*

By dying, Jesus defeats death. By taking on the shame of the cross, He puts the powers of evil to shame.

When we look at our humdrum lives, we may not feel as if we have entered into glory. Instead it looks more like the pain, shame, and defeat of hanging on a cross. We may have resigned ourselves to that loss as the best life we can hope for.

But God through Christ has snatched victory from defeat. By faith we see the King of Glory, the all-time winner, the Conqueror of all, enter into us as His holy temple. All He asks is that we enter His presence with a single will and a pure heart.

For Reflection

1. What comes to mind when you think of the word "glory"?

2. How do we glorify God?

3. How is the cross a victory and not a defeat?

Living the Messiah

1. In all you do today, think of how your actions bring you to the glory of God.

2. Try to capture the feeling you have when your sports team wins and feel the same elation at your victory in Jesus.

Prayer

Triumphant Jesus, may we seek your glory with all our hearts this day. With your presence in us, let us glorify you and serve others.

DAY TWENTY-ONE:
WORSHIP

Unto which of the angels said He at any time, Thou art My Son, this day have I begotten Thee? Let all the angels of God worship Him. *Hebrews 1:5-6*

When I think of worship I think of going to church. There we meet in a worship center where a worship leader guides us in acts of worship, but worship is more than that. Yes, we assemble with other Christians to worship the Lord, but the Bible says that worship involves every moment of our lives.

> **And so, dear brothers and sisters, I plead with you to give your bodies to God because of all he has done for you. Let them be a living and holy sacrifice—the kind he will find acceptable. This is truly the way to worship him.** *Romans 12:1*

If we give our bodies to God, then we worship with everything we do.

Worship then is like love. Yes, love is an action. We can rightly speak of acts of love. Yet we also say we fall in love. Love is not just something we do; it overwhelms us and becomes part of us. Love is in us all the time when we are in love.

Angels Worship

So we come back to angels worshipping Jesus. Earlier we looked at the angels who praised God at the birth of Jesus. After singing of the birth, suffering, and death of Jesus, *Messiah* returns to that theme. The angels worship Jesus in His death and glory, even before the resurrection.

The first quotation from Hebrews 1:5, "You are my Son. Today I have become your Father," is from Psalm 2:7. In the psalm, it is the king, likely David, whom God calls His son. Although it sounds strange to us, it was commonplace in the culture of David's time for people to think of kings as children of gods. The Lord often calls Israel as a whole His "child." Since the Lord is the real King of Israel, it is not a leap to think of God in a spiritual and political sense giving birth to His anointed king.

That is the near meaning of the verse. Christians rightly heard it as speaking of Jesus as the ultimate King of the Jews and the only begotten Son of God. The point of these words in the book of Hebrews is that Jesus is vastly superior to angels.

"And let all of God's angels worship him," is from the Song of Moses in Deuteronomy 32:43. It is difficult to know what these words mean in the context of Deuteronomy. They are in the Greek translation but not in the traditional Hebrew text. However, the meaning in the book of Hebrews is clear. Since Jesus is superior to angels and equal to the Lord God, the angels worship Him.

Worshipping Jesus

The angels are not the only ones who worship Jesus while He is on the earth. Many see that He has the power of God and is worthy of their worship. This is particularly significant because most of those who worship Jesus are Jews who believe they should worship no one but the Lord God, as in the first of the Ten Commandments.

The wise men bow down and worship the infant Jesus (Matthew 2:11). The disciples in the boat with Jesus worship Him when He calms a storm (Matthew 14:33). A Gentile woman worships Jesus even before He casts a demon from her daughter (Matthew 15:25). A blind man, healed by Jesus, worships Him (John 9:38). When a Roman military officer sees how Jesus dies, He worships (Luke 23:47).

Those who saw the resurrected Jesus worshipped Him (Matthew 28:9, 17; Luke 23:47, 24:52, John 20:28). After His ascension, Christians continue to worship Him (Acts 13:2). We are encouraged to "worship Christ as Lord of your life" (1 Peter 3:15).

Worshipping with Angels

That angels worship Jesus is especially amazing, since angels themselves are celestial beings so majestic that humans are tempted to worship them (Revelation 19:10, 22:8-9, Colossians 2:18). We join with the angels in a great assembly of praise to Jesus.

> **No, you have come to Mount Zion, to the city of the living God, the heavenly Jerusalem, and to countless thousands of angels in a joyful gathering. You have come to the assembly of God's firstborn children, whose names are written in heaven. You have come to God himself, who is the judge over all things. You have come to the spirits of the righteous ones in heaven who have now been made perfect. You have come to Jesus, the one who mediates the new covenant between God and people, and to the sprinkled blood, which speaks of forgiveness instead of crying out for vengeance like the blood of Abel.** *Hebrews 12:22-24*

The writer of Hebrews contrasts the terrifying assembly of Israel at Mount Sinai (Hebrews 12:18-21, Exodus 19:12-23) where the Lord threatened to destroy Israel because of their idolatry (Deuteronomy 9:19) with an assembly overflowing with joy.

Who is at this great assembly? Countless angels. The firstborn children of God. We who trust in Jesus are all firstborn children who receive a full inheritance. The assembly includes those believers who have died and gone to be with the Lord. And what are angels and those faithful, living and dead, doing in this great assembly? They are worshiping the Lord God and Jesus the Mediator and High Priest.

When we go to church to worship, it is never a mundane gathering. We are not only there with the brothers and sisters we know so well. Those who have gone before us are still with us in spirit in that assembly. A host of angels is praising Jesus with us. We are in the very presence of the Lord God—Father, Son, and Spirit.

Worship to Come

Note that these words from Hebrews are in the past tense. We have already come to Mount Zion, and have already joined this great assembly of praise. This happens not only when we go to church to worship, but this great assembly infuses every moment of our lives as we give our bodies in worship to Jesus. Our minds and hearts are already in heaven.

> **Since you have been raised to new life with Christ, set your sights on the realities of heaven, where Christ sits in the place of honor at God's right hand. Think about the things of heaven, not the things of earth.** *Colossians 3:1-2*

Yet the worship we experience now is just an appetizer for the eternal praise we will enjoy

> **No longer will there be a curse upon anything. For the throne of God and of the Lamb will be there, and his servants will worship him. And they will see his face, and**

his name will be written on their foreheads. And there will be no night there—no need for lamps or sun—for the Lord God will shine on them. And they will reign forever and ever. *Revelation 22:3-5*

For Reflection

1. Why might one be tempted to worship an angel?

2. Why do the angels worship Jesus?

3. Look back at the stories of people worshipping Jesus during His ministry. What did Jesus do that called for their worship?

Living the Messiah

1. When you next go to church, imagine angels and the spirits of departed Christians joining you in praise.

2. Visualize the daily tasks of life as worship.

Prayer

Lord Jesus, Creator, King of the Universe, Ruler of angels, we give you praise with every breath we take! Thanks you for inviting us into your great assembly of worship.

DAY TWENTY-TWO:
RESCUE

Thou art gone up on high, Thou hast led captivity captive, and received gifts for men; yea, even for Thine enemies, that the Lord God might dwell among them.
Psalm 68:18

Hostages taken in war are in the news again. War causes so many tragedies, but none are worse than kidnapping innocent non-combatants and holding them as bargaining chips in the conflict. No hostage escapes without trauma. Some do not escape with their lives.

That's why the daring rescue mission that frees the captives so moves us.

Gone Up

The words from Psalm 68 portray the Lord as a warrior that frees captives. The passage begins by saying God has "gone up on high." Some associate these words with the time David brought the Ark of the Covenant to Mount Zion (2 Samuel 6:12-19). The Ark always symbolized the triumph of the Lord over His enemies. Even in the wilderness, Israel moved the Ark with these words, "Arise, O Lord, and let your enemies be scattered! Let them flee before you!" (Numbers 10:35). To "go up on high" might simply be a metaphor for winning battles, since we still talk of victory "over" our foes. The point is that the Lord is mighty in battle (Psalm 24:8). The Old Testament is full of stories of God fighting for His people.

Paul quotes Psalm 68:18 and applies the words to Jesus:

> **That is why the Scriptures say,**
> **"When he ascended to the heights,**
> **he led a crowd of captives**
> **and gave gifts to his people."**
> **Notice that it says "he ascended." This clearly means**
> **that Christ also descended to our lowly world. And the**
> **same one who descended is the one who ascended**
> **higher than all the heavens, so that he might fill the entire**
> **universe with himself.** *Ephesians 4:8-9*

As the Lord God fought for His people Israel and gave them the victory, so Jesus has won the battle against evil. Jesus also "went up" or ascended. This could refer to His ascension back to glory after the resurrection (Acts 1:9-11) or to His rising up from the empty tomb. However, in the singing of *Messiah* we have not yet reached the story of the resurrection. The going up here is likely the lifting up of Jesus on the cross.

> **"And when I am lifted up from the earth, I will draw**
> **everyone to myself." He said this to indicate how he was**
> **going to die.** *John 12:32-33*

When Jesus died on the cross, it looked like defeat but instead it was the glorious victory over evil and death, a triumph that drew everyone to salvation.

Capturing the Captives

After winning a war, home crowds joyfully welcomed the conquering heroes who often led a parade of plunder and captives. Think of the celebrations at the end of World War II. This happens in the Old Testament when the Lord gives His people victory (Judges 5:12). The captives on parade may be enemies taken in battle or they may be hostages, former captives, who have been rescued.

The Lord God and Jesus as Lord have brought an end to captivity itself. The death of Jesus on the cross set us free from the slavery of sin. On the cross, Jesus defeated the powers of evil and death.

You were dead because of your sins and because your sinful nature was not yet cut away. Then God made you alive with Christ, for he forgave all our sins. He canceled the record of the charges against us and took it away by nailing it to the cross. In this way, he disarmed the spiritual rulers and authorities. He shamed them publicly by his victory over them on the cross. *Colossians 2:13-15*

Jesus turned what was meant to be a shameful death, crucifixion of a criminal, into a shameful defeat of our enemies. Jesus rescues us from captivity by capturing us for Himself. He does not make us hostages by force, but captures our hearts and lives through His sacrificial love. We are happy to be captives of Christ!

But thank God! He has made us his captives and continues to lead us along in Christ's triumphal procession. *2 Corinthians 2:14*

We join in the great victory parade of God through Christ, thankful that He has made us His own.

Gifts

Rulers usually share the spoils of war with their people. Victory leads to gift giving. So Jesus, having gone up on high, gives gifts to benefit the church.

> **Now these are the gifts Christ gave to the church: the apostles, the prophets, the evangelists, and the pastors and teachers. Their responsibility is to equip God's people to do his work and build up the church, the body of Christ. This will continue until we all come to such unity in our faith and knowledge of God's Son that we will be mature in the Lord, measuring up to the full and complete standard of Christ.** *Ephesians 4:11-13*

Having won the war, Jesus now equips us to live lives of peace. Messiah gives more than forgiveness from sin. He gives us spiritual gifts so that we may bless others, supplying them with everything they need to be mature Christians.

Enemies

Jesus won the victory over His spiritual enemies so He could save those who had made themselves His enemies. Even on the cross, He prayed "Father, forgive them" (Luke 23:34). Jesus died for the very people who put Him on the cross. His rescue is for all. He even died for us when we were enemies.

> **For since our friendship with God was restored by the death of his Son while we were still his enemies, we will certainly be saved through the life of his Son.** *Romans 5:10*

What a complete victory! Jesus goes up on high in triumph over His enemies. He frees those who are captive. He captures us as His own possession, parading us in victory before the world. He shares the spoils of His victory with us. He rescues even His enemies.

For Reflection

1. What would it feel like to be a hostage in a war? How were we hostages to sin? How did that feel?

2. What are the different ways that Jesus has "gone up on high"?

3. What is the purpose of the gifts Jesus gives? How might that change how we look at those gifts?

Living the Messiah

1. As you pray today, feel yourself lifted up on high with God and Jesus.

2. Through the power of Jesus, help someone in your life who needs rescuing.

Prayer

Lord, we lift your Name on high, praising you for rescuing us through the death of Jesus. May we use the gifts you give us to rescue others.

DAY TWENTY-THREE:
PREACHERS

The Lord gave the word; great was the company of the preachers. *Psalm 68:11*

How beautiful are the feet of them that preach the gospel of peace, and bring glad tidings of good things! *Isaiah 52:7; Romans 10:15*

Their sound is gone out into all lands, and their words unto the ends of the world. *Psalm 19:4; Romans 10:18*

I confess that I am a preacher. For most of my life I have preached and trained others to preach.

I am reluctant to tell people that I am a preacher. I don't think I'm ashamed of Jesus or the gospel, but when people find out that I preach, they react in predictable ways. They apologize for the bad words they use. Or they want me to solve some religious argument they have with someone. Or they go on a rant on how religion has caused all the problems of the world.

My biggest problem is that when they find out I am a preacher, they don't treat me like a real human being anymore. I'm either superhuman or subhuman.

That's why this part of *Messiah,* with its joy in preaching, is one of my favorites.

Victory

The great company of the preachers is in the context of Psalm 68 which praises the Lord as the conquering King. What's interesting is that the word for preacher or proclaimer here is feminine. "The Lord announces the word, and the women who proclaim it are a mighty throng"

Women celebrate the Lord's victories throughout the Bible. Miriam, Moses' sister, who is a prophet, sings a victory song praising the Lord for their deliverance from Pharaoh (Genesis 15:20-21). Deborah the judge composes a song of gratitude for God's triumph over the Canaanites (Judges 5:1-31). Women sing and dance for joy at the success of Saul and David in battle (1 Samuel 18:6-7). When the angel Gabriel tells Mary she will have a child who will be the Savior, she breaks into a hymn of praise, the Magnificat, that speaks of God as a conquering hero.

> **His mighty arm has done tremendous things!**
> **He has scattered the proud and haughty ones.**
> **He has brought down princes from their thrones**
> **and exalted the humble.** *Luke 1:51-52*

And women are the first to announce the greatest victory of all, the triumph of Jesus over death through his resurrection (Luke 24:10-11). But the men would not believe their news!

The great company of preachers includes all who celebrate what God has done. Women and men, ordained and lay, all proclaim the power and grace of the Lord. We are all preachers.

Good News

Isaiah says that even the feet of those who preach are beautiful. Isaiah never saw my feet. My heals are cracked, my toes have fungus, and my veins are red. Many of us like to hide our feet.

What makes the feet of the preachers beautiful is that they are running to spread good news. In Isaiah 52 the good news is that the Lord will redeem His people from exile. Paul uses this verse in Romans to speak of the even better news of the full redemption of humanity through Jesus.

This reminds me of the story of the first marathon. "Marathon" originally did not refer to a race but to the story of Pheidippides, an Athenian courier who, in 490 BC, ran from the battlefield at Marathon to tell those in Athens of their great victory over the Persians. After running over twenty-five miles, he breathlessly announces, "Rejoice! We conquer!" and immediately dies.

In the same way, proclaiming the great victory of God through Jesus demands every step we take, even our last breath. By word and deed we shout out the joyful news of conquest over sin and death.

Trusting the News

The Bible says this good news has gone or will go out to everyone in the whole earth. Psalm 19 says that the whole creation proclaims this good news.

> **The heavens proclaim the glory of God.**
> **The skies display his craftsmanship.**
> **Day after day they continue to speak;**
> **night after night they make him known.**
> **They speak without a sound or word;**
> **their voice is never heard.**
> **Yet their message has gone throughout the earth,**
> **and their words to all the world.** *Psalm 19:1-4*

Paul quotes these words in Romans to show that Israel has heard the good news about Christ (Romans 10:17-18). Did Paul mean that everyone in Israel and the world had heard the gospel? It doesn't appear so, since he says that he and others should continue to proclaim the good news. What Paul struggles with is why some in Israel and other nations would reject such news. From what they can see in creation, they should know and embrace a loving God.

Jesus died for all to reconcile them to God. Salvation is by grace. No one needs to earn it. And the good news is for everyone, no exceptions.

So why do some not believe this good news? It's not a new question.

But how can they call on him to save them unless they believe in him? And how can they believe in him if they have never heard about him? And how can they hear about him unless someone tells them? And how will anyone go and tell them without being sent? That is why the Scriptures say, "How beautiful are the feet of messengers who bring good news!"
But not everyone welcomes the Good News, for Isaiah the prophet said, "Lord, who has believed our message?"
So faith comes from hearing, that is, hearing the Good News about Christ. *Romans 10:14-17*

The good news is that Jesus saves all who call on Him. But they cannot ask Him for salvation unless they trust Him. And they cannot trust Him until they hear about Him. And they cannot hear unless someone tells them. And the preachers cannot proclaim the message of Jesus until someone sends them.

Saving faith comes from hearing the word of God, the good news about Jesus. But not all welcome the good news. Why? Why would anyone reject good news? Because they do not believe it. Perhaps they think the news is too good to be true. Maybe they are not willing to do what it takes to trust Jesus, not willing to surrender control of their lives.

Or do they reject the good news because of the messengers? The tragedy is that Christians have the reputation for spreading bad news, not good. "You are a sinner. You need to stop that and get your life straight before you can be right with God." To some, this is "gospel preaching." No wonder many think Christians are strict, condemning, and hypercritical, judging others before we even get to know them.

That is not the good news of Jesus. The gospel He announced was good news to the poor and oppressed (Luke 4:16-21). He ate with those others considered to be "sinners" (Matthew 9:10-13).

That is not the good news Paul preached. When he speaks to the philosophers' club at Mars Hill in Athens, he does not say that God is far from them, condemning them for their pagan immorality. Instead he announces that God is near them and reveals the God they were ignorantly worshipping (Acts 17:18-34).

God calls us to join the great company of the preachers. Jesus sends every Christian to tell the good news. We proclaim it each day when we show love for God and for our neighbors. Those around us see the good news in the joyful lives we lead. They see our good works and glorify God in heaven (Matthew 5:16). They trust the message because they trust us.

For Reflection

1. Why do you think God so often chooses women to tell others of His victory?

2. How is being a preacher, a teller of the good news, like being a marathon runner?

3. Why do some not believe the good news?

Living the Messiah

1. Think of yourself as a preacher today. How does that change how you live?

2. Live in such a way that those around you hear good news, not bad news.

Prayer

Jesus, open the ears of our hearts so we may hear you good news today. Open our eyes to see your salvation. May we speak and live this good news in a world that is desperate for it.

DAY TWENTY-FOUR:
REBELLION

Why do the nations so furiously rage together? and why do the people imagine a vain thing?

The kings of the earth rise up, and the rulers take counsel together against the Lord, and against His anointed.

Let us break their bonds asunder, and cast away their yokes from us.

He that dwelleth in Heaven shall laugh them to scorn; the Lord shall have them in derision.

Thou shalt break them with a rod of iron; Thou shalt dash them in pieces like a potter's vessel. *Psalm 2:1-4, 9*

The United States was born in rebellion. As a patriotic American, I think it was a legitimate rebellion against the tyranny of a king.

I also am a child of the South, raised to be proud of being a rebel. It wasn't until I was older that I learned that one thing the South was rebelling against in the Civil War was the right of anyone to curtail the practice of slavery. Yes, it's fine to be proud as a Southerner, but we dare not become rebels against justice and equality.

Most Americans prize the image of the rebel. However, what or who you rebel against makes all the difference.

Rebellion Against God

It is never a good idea to rebel against God. He is the source of all goodness and happiness. To reject God is to choose misery and death. It's also a bad idea because no one can successfully rebel against Him, the God of all Power, although the rebels may seem victorious for a time.

The story of the Bible is largely an account of rebellion against the Lord. It starts in the Garden of Eden where Adam and Eve buy the lie of the serpent that rejecting what God desires will make humans like God (Genesis 3:1-7). We want to be our own god. We want to run our own lives, with no one to tell us what to do. That is the basic human uprising against God. That rebellion becomes so widespread that the Lord starts humanity over with Noah and the Flood.

But God has a plan to not only defeat the rebellion but to save the rebels. He calls Abraham and promises to make his descendants a great nation that will bless all nations. Yet the story of Israel is the tale of constant revolt against the will of God. Even then, God does not abandon His people but sends judges, prophets, and even some kings to call them back to Him.

Yet the people often oppose the good kings, like the anointed one of Psalm 2. The kings of other nations war against Israel. The rebellion spreads.

Rebellion Against the Anointed One

The Lord's ultimate plan is to send another anointed King, the Messiah. Yet when that anointed Messiah comes, God's people and the kings of the earth oppose Him. "He came to his own people, and even they rejected him" (John 1:11). The religious leaders condemn Jesus and bring Him to Pilate, the representative of the Emperor, the king of the earth, for execution. Pilate crucifies Jesus on the charge that He is "King of the Jews" (John 19:19-22).

Why do kings reject Jesus? Because they see Him as a threat to their authority. King Herod kills the boy babies of Bethlehem because he hears a new King has been born there (Matthew 2:1-18). Caiaphas, the High Priest, says Jesus must die to prevent the Romans army from destroying Israel (John 11:47-50). Later, he and other priests say, "We have no king but Caesar" (John 19:15). Those who made sacrifices to the Lord joined the kings of the earth in rejecting the Lord's anointed.

The Lord Responds

How does the Lord respond to rebellion? He punishes in order to win his people back. He sends emissaries to call them back. But how does God react to the combined power of all the kingdoms of the earth?

He laughs. The rage of rebellious nations makes Him chuckle. "Puny human kings, you think you can threaten me? You've got to be kidding." That's what God says. The Almighty King of Kings has the last laugh at the empty imagination of those who think they can run their own lives and their own kingdoms. The Lord laughs because He holds all the cards. He has all the power. He can swat any despot like a fly. He can break them like the flimsiest pottery.

How does He break their insurrection? Does He call on His vast army of angels? Does He raise up an overwhelming human military force to conquer them? No! He wins the battle through His Anointed.

How does Jesus defeat the rulers lined up against Him? It looks as though they win when they nail Him to a cross, but the way He triumphs displays the nature of the kingdom of God. What kind of King is Jesus? That's what Pilate wants to know.

> Then Pilate went back into his headquarters and called for Jesus to be brought to him. "Are you the king of the Jews?" he asked him.
>
> Jesus replied, "Is this your own question, or did others tell you about me?"
>
> "Am I a Jew?" Pilate retorted. "Your own people and their leading priests brought you to me for trial. Why? What have you done?"
>
> Jesus answered, "My Kingdom is not an earthly kingdom. If it were, my followers would fight to keep me from being handed over to the Jewish leaders. But my Kingdom is not of this world."
>
> Pilate said, "So you are a king?"
>
> Jesus responded, "You say I am a king. Actually, I was born and came into the world to testify to the truth. All who love the truth recognize that what I say is true."
>
> *John 18:33-37*

Many misunderstand "my Kingdom is not an earthly kingdom" to mean that Jesus does not rule all the world, but only the spiritual or religious world. That cannot be true since Jesus has all "authority in heaven and earth" (Matthew 28:18). Jesus explains what He means by saying that if His kingdom were like others, "my followers would fight." The conquering Messiah destroys His rebellious enemies, not with physical violence, but through the sacrificial love of the cross. He defeats political kings and all who rebel against God by dying to reconcile them to the Father. The kingdom of the Messiah does not spread through the use of the sword, but through service to others, even enemies.

Who Rules?

The earliest Christians learned this lesson of the kingdom. They did not rebel against Rome, even when Roman authorities persecuted them unjustly. Instead, they suffered as Jesus did. They lived their quiet lives of service, helping those that Roman society would not assist. As a result, the Roman Empire eventually accepted Christianity.

The tragedy is that Christian Rome soon forgot the nature of the Messiah's kingdom and began to enforce conversion and conformity to Christian doctrine through violence and armies.

The choice is still with us today. Will we live in the kingdom of self-giving love or will we try to force the faith on others? If we choose the way of coercion, then we are rebels against the Lord and His Anointed. Psalm 2 gives a stark contrast between those who rebel and are crushed by the iron rod of God, and those who take refuge in the Lord in joy.

> **Submit to God's royal son, or he will become angry, and you will be destroyed in the midst of all your activities—**
> **for his anger flares up in an instant.**
> **But what joy for all who take refuge in him!** *Psalm 2:12*

In a world in rebellion against all that is good, we trust in the One who gave Himself for us to bring us eternal joy.

For Reflection

1. Why would humans rebel against a God of love?

2. Do kings, prime ministers, and presidents really run the world? Why does it look that way?

3. How should Christians fight for Jesus?

Living the Messiah

1. Live today as if Jesus, not the leaders of your country, rules your life.

2. Live today as if Jesus rules your life, not you.

Prayer

Almighty God and Suffering Messiah, give us the wisdom to live in your kingdom, not the kingdoms of the world. Forgive our rebellion! May we fight evil with the weapons of Jesus—service, healing, and truth.

DAY TWENTY-FIVE:
HALLELUJAH

**Hallelujah! for the Lord God Omnipotent reigneth.
The kingdom of this world is become the kingdom of
our Lord and of His Christ; and He shall reign forever
and ever.
King of Kings, and Lord of Lords.** *Revelation 11:15, 19:6*

For ten years I was part of an ecumenical organization that allowed me to see what God is doing in over twenty-five countries around the world. It was such a blessing to worship with Christians from various traditions, nationalities, and languages. I once attended a multi-day Christian conference with thousands of South Koreans where I only understood one word—"Hallelujah." But that one word and the joy in the faces of the worshippers were enough to enrapture my heart.

Praise the Name

No matter what language Christians worship in, they all share the Hebrew word "Hallelujah." It is a compound word, *hallelu*, translated "let us praise," and *jah* or *"yah"* the name of God. *"Yah"* is a shortened form of "Yahweh." After the Exile, Jews so reverenced this name for God that they stopped saying it, substituting the word "Lord" whenever they found the four consonants of God's Name, YHWH, in the Bible. Most Modern English translations now use LORD (in all caps) when translating this name and Lord (with only the first letter capitalized) for the general word for Lord.

If that sounds confusing, what puzzles many of us is that God would have a name. However, in a world where there were many "gods," God (the one true God) reveals Himself to Moses by name at the burning bush.

> **But Moses protested, "If I go to the people of Israel and tell them, 'The God of your ancestors has sent me to you,' they will ask me, 'What is his name?' Then what should I tell them?"**
> **God replied to Moses, "I am who I am. Say this to the people of Israel: I am has sent me to you." God also said to Moses, "Say this to the people of Israel: Yahweh, the God of your ancestors—the God of Abraham, the God of Isaac, and the God of Jacob—has sent me to you.**
> **This is my eternal name, my name to remember for all generations.** *Exodus 3:13-15*

Christians rarely use this name, Yahweh, for God, but when we say "God," our meaning is often unclear. Do we mean God the Father? Do we mean the Trinity—Father, Son, and Spirit?

The point of all this is that "Hallelujah" is not just a meaningless shout of praise. We are saying, "Let us praise Yahweh." We are lifting up the Holy Name of the God of Abraham, Isaac, and Jacob. We are praising Father, Son, and Spirit.

Praise the King

We praise the Name of the Lord simply because He is God. We also praise Him as the all-powerful King. As we have seen earlier in *Messiah*, other kings claim authority but God has defeated them all.

The Book of Revelation looks forward to that day when the conquest is complete.

> **Then the seventh angel blew his trumpet, and there were loud voices in heaven, saying, "The kingdom of the world has become the kingdom of our Lord and of his Christ, and he shall reign forever and ever." And the twenty-four elders who sit on their thrones before God fell on their faces and worshiped God, saying,**
> **"We give thanks to you, Lord God Almighty,**
> **who is and who was,**
> **for you have taken your great power**
> **and begun to reign.**
> **The nations raged,**
> **but your wrath came,**
> **and the time for the dead to be judged,**
> **and for rewarding your servants, the prophets and saints,**
> **and those who fear your name,**
> **both small and great,**
> **and for destroying the destroyers of the earth."**
> *Revelation 11:15-18 (ESV)*

Here are the original loud voices belting out the *Hallelujah Chorus*. They shout because the ultimate judgment of evil is at hand. The world, which in reality has always belonged to the Lord and His Messiah, now becomes their kingdom in the eyes and ears of everyone—angels, elders, and all. We join them in grateful praise that all the injustices of the world will be put right on the day of judgment and justice. May justice day come soon!

Praise the Lamb

The Book of Revelation portrays Jesus as "the Lamb who was slaughtered before the world was made" (Revelation 13:8). Messiah shows himself as King through self-sacrificial love on the cross. That love is so powerful that the blood of the Lamb enables God's people to defeat the "great dragon—the ancient serpent called the devil, or Satan" (Revelation 12:8-11).

We praise Jesus as the Messiah, the Lamb of God who takes away the sins of the world. We also praise Him because He has taken us, the church, as His bride.

> **Then I heard what seemed to be the voice of a great multitude, like the roar of many waters and like the sound of mighty peals of thunder, crying out,**
> **"Hallelujah!**
> **For the Lord our God**
> **the Almighty reigns.**
> **Let us rejoice and exult**
> **and give him the glory,**
> **for the marriage of the Lamb has come,**
> **and his Bride has made herself ready;**
> **it was granted her to clothe herself**
> **with fine linen, bright and pure"—**
> **for the fine linen is the righteous deeds of the saints.**
> *Revelation 19:6-8 (ESV)*

When the Bible speaks of the closeness of our relationship with Jesus, it compares it to the most intimate human relationship—a committed marriage. We are already the bride of Christ (Ephesians 5:25-27), but that bond reaches its apex in the great marriage ceremony and wedding feast to come.

Praise with our Bodies

We shout "Hallelujah!" We sing "Hallelujah." We praise the Lord not just with our voices but with our bodies.

When the choir sings the *Hallelujah Chorus*, everyone stands. The story (which may not be true) is that the *Hallelujah Chorus* so moved King George II at the premier of *Messiah* in London that he stood in reverence. When the king stood, everyone stood. Audiences have been standing ever since.

True or not, the story shows how one monarch may have recognized the King of Kings and Lord of Lords. When we recognize the Lord and His Messiah, we stand in respect, kneel in humility, and sometimes throw ourselves face down in awe. We glorify God in our bodies. We live the Hallelujah. Let us praise the Lord!

For Reflection

1. What was your reaction when you first heard the *Hallelujah Chorus*?

2. How is Jesus already king? How is He not yet king?

3. What comes to mind when you think of a bride? How does that affect your view of your relationship with Jesus?

Living the Messiah

1. In your time alone with God, call Him by Name.

2. In private, stand, raise hands, kneel, and fall face down as you shout "hallelujah."

Prayer

Praise be to Yahweh, our King! Praise be to Christ, the Lamb, our Husband! Reign over us forever! Hallelujah!

DAY TWENTY-SIX:
REDEEMER

I know that my Redeemer liveth, and that He shall stand at the latter day upon the earth.
And though worms destroy this body, yet in my flesh shall I see God. *Job 19:25–26*

Have you ever known you were right when everyone else thought you were wrong? So many were against you that you began to doubt yourself. Then an amazing thing happened. Someone else came to your defense. More than that, they proved you right, vindicating you in front of those who had doubted.

Job's Redeemer

That's the hope that Job has, but Job needs more than to be proven right in an argument. He needs someone to show that he is right before God.

Let's review the Job story. The Lord Himself describes Job as "the finest man in all the earth. He is blameless—a man of complete integrity. He fears God and stays away from evil" (Job 1:8). Satan, the Accuser, says that Job only serves the Lord because of the protection and prosperity that God has given. The Lord then gives Satan permission to test Job's integrity by taking everything from him—all his wealth, family, and health. Job is left with nothing but his life.

Why did the Lord allow this to happen to Job? We, the readers of Job, know it is a test but Job does not know that. Why would a just God bring such disaster on a blameless man?

Job's wife knows her husband. She can only blame God for all the trouble that has happened to Job, thinking the Lord to be an unfair and evil God. She therefore tells Job to "curse God and die" (Job 2:9). But Job maintains his relationship to God, even though Job does not understand why all this is happening to him.

Job's friends arrive and try to comfort him by sitting in silence with him for seven days. "They saw that his suffering was too great for words" (Job 2:13). But then they open their mouths. They want to defend God. They know that God is fair, so Job must have done something to deserve this terrible punishment. Job maintains his innocence. That does not mean that Job thought he was sinless, only that he knew he had not done anything to deserve this rough treatment from God.

The bulk of the book of Job is a series of conversations between Job and his friends. The friends condemn Job so harshly that he calls them "miserable comforters" (Job 16:2). They wear Job out with their bitter accusations. What Job wants more than anything is for someone to take his side. He needs a defender, a fair judge.

But who can defend Job before the Almighty? Who can resolve the conflict between Job and his accusers? Only God himself.

So in an astounding show of trust, Job calls on God to redeem him.

> **"But as for me, I know that my Redeemer lives,**
> **and he will stand upon the earth at last.**
> **And after my body has decayed,**

yet in my body I will see God!
I will see him for myself.
Yes, I will see him with my own eyes.
I am overwhelmed at the thought!" *Job 19:25-27*

The word for "redeemer" here has a rich heritage in the Old Testament. It refers to a relative who brings justice to a difficult situation. The "redeemer" buys back property for a relative (Leviticus 25:25-27) and frees an enslaved relative (Leviticus 25:48–49). Redeemers even take vengeance on those who murder their family members (Num 35:12-27). The Book of Ruth is a story of Boaz who redeems the property of a relative by marrying his widow, Ruth, and providing a livelihood for her and her mother-in-law Naomi.

In spite of all that God had allowed to happen to him, Job still views God as close to him, his next of kin. He is confident that he will see God and that God will vindicate him. And that is what happens! God appears to Job in a whirlwind, overwhelming him with His Presence and reminding Job how small he is. Job cannot fathom the Lord (Job 38:1-41:34). Yet the lord vindicates Job over his friends, "After the Lord had finished speaking to Job, he said to Eliphaz the Temanite: 'I am angry with you and your two friends, for you have not spoken accurately about me, as my servant Job has'" (Job 42:7).

Jesus' Redeemer

Although the New Testament does not quote these words from Job, they could easily be the words of Jesus as He faced the cross. We often speak of faith in Jesus but rarely about the faith of Jesus. As fully human, Jesus had to trust that God the Father would redeem Him from death. Like Job, Jesus is suffering unjustly. Like Job, He wants the suffering to go away. In Gethsemane He prays, "My Father! If it is possible, let this cup of suffering be taken away from me." Yet, like Job, Jesus trusts in the goodness of the Father, even when He cannot see it, "Yet I want your will to be done, not mine" (Matthew 26:39).

On the cross, Jesus is sure that He will be with God in paradise. That certainty came through faith. Jesus trusted not only that His soul would be with God after His death but also that the Father would raise Him from the dead (Matthew 16:21, 17:22-23, 20:18-19, 27:63; Mark 8:31, 9:31, 10:33-34, 14:28; Luke 9:22, 18:31-33, 24:6-7; and John 2:19-22). Jesus knew that God His Redeemer lived and that in His resurrected body He would see God again.

We are therefore saved through faith in Jesus, but also though His faith, His trust in God.

Our Redeemer

We also can sing, "I know that my Redeemer lives," singing of Jesus the Messiah who redeemed us from sin. He is our near relative, the kinsman who pays the debt for us, buying us back from slavery. He is our brother, like us in every way (Hebrews 2:11-18, Mark 3:33-34).

We also can sing of seeing God in the flesh. We not only believe our spirits go to be with God at death, but we believe that our bodies will be resurrected at the Second Coming of Jesus (1 Corinthians 15:12-58). If alive at His coming, our bodies will be changed.

> **We tell you this directly from the Lord: We who are still living when the Lord returns will not meet him ahead of those who have died. For the Lord himself will come down from heaven with a commanding shout, with the voice of the archangel, and with the trumpet call of God. First, the believers who have died will rise from their graves. Then, together with them, we who are still alive and remain on the earth will be caught up in the clouds to meet the Lord in the air. Then we will be with the Lord forever. So encourage each other with these words.** *1 Thessalonians 4:15-16*

In a world where those around us constantly say that faith makes no sense, who tell us to curse God and die, we need one who will defend us. Like Job, we need a Redeemer. Facing our own Gethsemane, we need, like Jesus, to put our faith in the One who will never abandon us. His will be done. When our body begins to break down and we face our own death, we can say with confidence, "I know that my Redeemer lives! In my resurrected flesh, I will see God." We will see our Redeemer face to face for all eternity.

For Reflection

1. Why is Job's faith in God as Redeemer so amazing?

2. Why is the faith of Jesus in God, even from the cross, so amazing?

3. What gets in the way of our trust in Jesus as our Redeemer?

Living the Mesiah

1. Live this day in confidence that Jesus has fully redeemed you from sin and guilt.

2. Perform a redemptive act for someone today, paying the price to help them.

Prayer

Redeemer, give us confidence in our redemption. Thank you for being on our side when it looks like everyone is against us. Your will be done.

DAY TWENTY-SEVEN:
HUMAN

For now is Christ risen from the dead, the firstfruits of them that sleep.
Since by man came death, by man came also the resurrection of the dead. For as in Adam all die, even so in Christ shall all be made alive. *I Corinthians 15:20–22*

"I'm only human."

We've all heard that. We've likely said it ourselves.

"I'm only human."

When we say these words, we are not thinking of all the marvelous accomplishments of humanity. We are not bragging of the selfless acts of countless humans who gave themselves for others.

No. "Only human" is our way of admitting our limitations, our brokenness, and our almost infinite ability to mess things up. "I'm only human" means "Cut me some slack. You know what people are like."

Original Humanity

But we believe that God made human beings. Could He do no better than this? Did He create us to be the flawed and tragic people we are? Many think so, and blame God for all the evil that humans do.

The Bible tells a different story. In the beginning, God created the world and said it was good. He made humans, male and female, from the dust of the earth. He placed them in a beautiful garden and asked them to care for it. He gave them the Tree of Life so they might eat and live forever. The Lord himself walked with them in the garden (see Genesis 1-3).

God's original intent was that humans would live in harmony with one another and with the rest of creation. God wanted an intimate relationship with these humans, talking with them as His own.

How wonderful to be merely human!

> When I look at the night sky and see the work of your fingers—
> the moon and the stars you set in place—
> what are mere mortals that you should think about them,
> human beings that you should care for them?
> Yet you made them only a little lower than God
> and crowned them with glory and honor.
> You gave them charge of everything you made,
> putting all things under their authority—
> the flocks and the herds,
> and all the wild animals,
> the birds in the sky, the fish in the sea,
> and everything that swims the ocean currents.
> O Lord, our Lord,
> your majestic name fills the earth!
> *Psalm 8:3-9*

This is what the Lord intended for us to be.

Fallen Humanity

Then it all went wrong. The one thing the Lord told Adam and Eve to avoid was eating of the Tree of Knowledge. Instead, they listened to the deceptive words of the serpent, ate the fruit, and discovered the power of evil. As a result, the Lord banished them from the garden and the Tree of Life. Death entered the world, not just for humans, but for all creation. With death came decay, pain, and violence. The first sin in the Bible is eating forbidden fruit. The second is the deliberate murder of a brother (Genesis 4:8). Soon violence became so widespread that God starts humanity anew through the Flood and Noah (Genesis 6:9-13). That restart did not make humanity what God intended, as we see throughout history with its wars, disasters, and oppression.

Who is to blame for what humans became? God? Could He not have made us to be always good? But if He had, we would not be human. To be human is to have choices. And if God gives us choices, then we are able to choose the deadly path.

If God is not to blame, who is? Adam is to blame.

> **When Adam sinned, sin entered the world. Adam's sin brought death, so death spread to everyone, for everyone sinned.** *Romans 5:12*

"In Adam's fall, we sinned all." Does that mean we have no responsibility for sin? Can we simply say, "Adam made we do it"? No. When Adam (the name means "Human") sinned, all humanity sinned with him. Yet we must admit that we choose to sin. The sin rate is 100%, that is, every human eventually takes the path away from God.

So Adam's sin is both unlike and like ours. He sinned in paradise. We sin in a fallen world consumed with anger and violence. He faced a simple choice—to eat or not to eat. Our choices are more difficult, with more gray areas than black and white. Yet, like Adam, we often choose to do what seems pleasant to us instead of what pleases God.

Like Adam, we listen to the deceiver who tells us we can be our own gods.

From the first rebellion in the garden until today, to be "only human" means we are not the way that God intended us to be. This was not His plan for Adam and for humanity. But God has always had a plan to put things right.

Renewed Humanity

God's plan was to restore humanity to what He wanted it to be from the beginning. To create a new humanity, God Himself took on flesh in Jesus. Jesus is the new human, the one who chose to obey God at every fork in the road. Through His life of obedience, His sacrificial death, and His triumphant resurrection, Jesus begins a new humanity.

> **But there is a great difference between Adam's sin and God's gracious gift. For the sin of this one man, Adam, brought death to many. But even greater is God's wonderful grace and his gift of forgiveness to many through this other man, Jesus Christ. And the result of God's gracious gift is very different from the result of that one man's sin. For Adam's sin led to condemnation, but God's free gift leads to our being made right with God, even though we are guilty of many sins. For the sin of this one man, Adam, caused death to rule over many. But even greater is God's wonderful grace and his gift of righteousness, for all who receive it will live in triumph over sin and death through this one man, Jesus Christ.**
> **Yes, Adam's one sin brings condemnation for everyone, but Christ's one act of righteousness brings a right relationship with God and new life for everyone. Because one person disobeyed God, many became sinners. But because one other person obeyed God, many will be made righteous.** *Romans 5:15-19*

The resurrection of Jesus is more than His body coming back to life. It is the resurrection of all humanity.

> **So you see, just as death came into the world through a man, now the resurrection from the dead has begun through another man. Just as everyone dies because we all belong to Adam, everyone who belongs to Christ will be given new life.** *1 Corinthians 15:21-22*

Living as New Humanity

What we lost in Adam we gain in Christ. Jesus takes away shame, guilt, sin, and death. He restores us to the paradise where we live in harmony with other people, the created order, and with God. The Lord again walks and talks with us as His own.

So now we can say, "I'm only human, only the way that God wants me to be through Christ." And the day will come when we join all of the new humanity in the New Jerusalem where the Tree of Life gives healing to the nations and we see God face-to-face (Revelation 22:1-4).

For Reflection

1. How are Adam's sin and our sin connected?

2. Why is God not to blame for the evil humans do?

3. How is Jesus the beginning of a new humanity?

Living the Messiah

1. Face the violence, injustice, and oppression around you with trust that this is not the way God intended things to be.

2. Through the Spirit in you, show the New Humanity of love to those you meet.

Prayer

Jesus, our new Adam, restore the image of God in us so we may proclaim the new life all have through you.

DAY TWENTY-EIGHT:
CHANGED

Behold, I tell you a mystery; we shall not all sleep, but we shall all be changed. In a moment, in the twinkling of an eye, at the last trumpet.
The trumpet shall sound, and the dead shall be raised incorruptible, and we shall be changed. For this corruptible must put on incorruption; and this mortal must put on immortality. *I Corinthians 15:51–53*

People don't change.

That's what others tell me. It's also what I've witnessed.

Or if they change they do it slowly. Have you ever tried to lose weight? It seems to take forever. Change in our bodies happens so slowly. The same is true of our personalities and character. Yes, a self-improvement program might eventually pay off, but do we have the willpower to see it through?

What if we could change for the better in an instant? What if someone changed every part of us—body, mind, and spirit?

Asleep

The change we dread the most is death, the final change. Yet when Jesus spoke of death, he often called it sleep. Jairus asks Jesus to heal his dying daughter. By the time Jesus arrives at his house, the news comes that the daughter is dead.

> Get out!" he told them. "The girl isn't dead; she's only asleep." But the crowd laughed at him. After the crowd was put outside, however, Jesus went in and took the girl by the hand, and she stood up! *Matthew 9:24-25*

It happens again when Jesus goes to raise Lazarus. In this case, the disciples do not laugh at Jesus, but they do misunderstand.

> Then he said, "Our friend Lazarus has fallen asleep, but now I will go and wake him up."
> The disciples said, "Lord, if he is sleeping, he will soon get better!" They thought Jesus meant Lazarus was simply sleeping, but Jesus meant Lazarus had died.
> *John 11:12-13*

What does Jesus mean by calling death "sleep"? He did not mean that death was not real. The girl and Lazarus were truly dead. What He means is that death is not permanent. Like sleep, we wake from it by the power of the resurrection.

This hope of the resurrection caused early Christians to adopt this language of sleep for death. When Stephen dies as a martyr, it says he "fell asleep" (Acts 7:59). Paul also speaks this way in 1 Corinthians 15 and 1 Thessalonians 4.

When we stand at the grave of someone we deeply love and see their body lowered into the ground, it seems so final, but we believe they will awake, that death does not have the last word. As the poet John Donne wrote:

Death, be not proud, though some have called thee

Mighty and dreadful, for thou art not so;

For those whom thou think'st thou dost overthrow

Die not, poor Death, nor yet canst thou kill me

One short sleep past, we wake eternally

And death shall be no more; Death, thou shalt die.

Changed

What a great comfort, to know that those who are dead are only sleeping. But Paul has an even more amazing truth to share. Some of us will not die at all. We will be alive when Jesus returns.

But what will happen to those of us alive at His coming? Can we enter into the new heaven and earth as we are? No!

> **What I am saying, dear brothers and sisters, is that our physical bodies cannot inherit the Kingdom of God. These dying bodies cannot inherit what will last forever.**
> *1 Corinthians 15:50*

So will our bodies die when Jesus returns? No! Instead He will change them so they become like His resurrected body.

> **He will take our weak mortal bodies and change them into glorious bodies like his own, using the same power with which he will bring everything under his control.**
> *Philippians 3:21*

We shall be changed! Immediately! In the twinkling of an eye.

And what a change! From corruptible to incorruptible. When I was young, I didn't appreciate those words as much as I do now. My body is certainly corruptible. I'm slowly falling apart. Whatever does not ache seems to itch. None of us get younger, but Jesus will return and make us forever young.

Mortal will put on immortality. Death is not the end. Jesus has defeated it.

> **For Christ must reign until he humbles all his enemies beneath his feet. And the last enemy to be destroyed is death.** *I Corinthians 15:25-26*

So in this death-dealing world of bombs and bullets, of hunger and plague, of anger and despair, we cry out in trust, "Lord, come quickly!" We shall be changed.

For Reflection

1. Do you find it hard to think of death as sleep? Why or why not?

2. What would you most like to change about yourself?

3. What makes us look forward to the coming of Jesus?

Living the Messiah

1. Pay attention to the "corruption" of your body today. Use that to help you look forward to your incorruptible body.

2. Live today as if Jesus is coming soon.

Prayer

Jesus, Resurrection and Life, as we face death, give us assurance of awakening with you. Come quickly Lord, so that we may never die.

DAY TWENTY-NINE:
VICTORY

Then shall be brought to pass the saying that is written, Death is swallowed up in victory.

O death, where is thy sting? O grave, where is thy victory? The sting of death is sin, and the strength of sin is the law.

But thanks be to God, Who giveth us the victory through our Lord Jesus Christ. *I Corinthians 15:54-57*

I've always been afraid of death.

It started in my childhood. I did not really understand death, but it was one of many childish fears. As I got older, I started paying attention to sermons that tried to motivate obedience through fear of hell. I was certainly afraid of hell.

Even now, although I am confident of missing hell, I am still afraid at the thought that I might somehow cease to exist at death. Can it be that all my memories, all the joys of living, that everything that makes "me" would be lost forever?

Is death the end?

Christ is Risen

I am a Christians, so why do I fear death? Don't I believe that God raised Jesus from the dead?

I do. I believe in the resurrection of Jesus. I believe in the whole story—empty tomb, appearances, and ascension. I believe for many reasons. Because others taught me this from infancy. Because of the testimony of the Bible. Because people I trust also believe. But most of all, because of the presence of the resurrected Jesus in my life.

I believe in the resurrection of Jesus. It's my own resurrection and the resurrection of those I love that I doubt. Which makes me much like the Corinthians. Paul had brought them the good news of the resurrection of Jesus, but now they saw their loved ones die and it looked so final. They began to doubt that they would see those they loved again.

So Paul writes them to show first that Jesus was raised from the dead. That was the good news Paul preached to them.

> **I passed on to you what was most important and what had also been passed on to me. Christ died for our sins, just as the Scriptures said. He was buried, and he was raised from the dead on the third day, just as the Scriptures said.** *1 Corinthians 15:3-4*

Paul then says that trust in the resurrection of Jesus gives us confidence of our own resurrection.

> **But in fact, Christ has been raised from the dead. He is the first of a great harvest of all who have died.** *1 Corinthians 15:20*

Pitied?

When it comes to believing in their own resurrections, Paul and the early Christians have an advantage over me. They longed for a better life. In this life, they faced hunger, pain, and persecution. When those in authority throw you in jail, beat you, confiscate your possessions, and threaten to kill you, then resurrection is particularly sweet. A better life is coming.

But if there is no resurrection, then all that suffering has no meaning.

> **And why should we ourselves risk our lives hour by hour? For I swear, dear brothers and sisters, that I face death daily. This is as certain as my pride in what Christ Jesus our Lord has done in you. And what value was there in fighting wild beasts—those people of Ephesus—if there will be no resurrection from the dead? And if there is no resurrection, "Let's feast and drink, for tomorrow we die!"**
>
> **And if Christ has not been raised, then your faith is useless and you are still guilty of your sins. In that case, all who have died believing in Christ are lost! And if our hope in Christ is only for this life, we are more to be pitied than anyone in the world.** *1 Corinthians 15:30-32, 17-19*

My problem is that I have it so good in this life. I've been blessed with good health. I'm never known hunger. I don't know what it's like to be homeless. I live in a house that is warm in the winter and cool in the summer. Yes, I've worked for a living, but the good life I enjoy is due more to being born into the middle class of a prosperous country than in my hard work. It's hard for me to look forward to the new heaven and earth when this earth has been so good. Even if death is the end, I don't feel I should be pitied.

I don't think I'm alone in this. Those who are poor and oppressed find it easier to put their hope in a better world, a resurrection world.

So what should we comfortable Christians do? I do not think we should pray for persecution. Instead we pray, "deliver us from evil." Perhaps we need to embrace more discomfort for the sake of the good news. And we need to trust that the world to come will be even more wonderful than the world we enjoy now.

How Raised?

Which brings me to my second barrier to trust in my resurrection. I wonder, *What will it be like?* It is not so much lack of faith that troubles me, but lack of imagination.

In this new heaven and earth, this resurrection land, will we have bodies? What age will we be? Will we recognize those we knew? Will our relationships be the same? Will I still be me?

The Bible does not give us clear answers on these and other similar questions. I'm not questioning the inspiration and authority of the Scriptures. They don't tell us because we cannot comprehend. So Paul says our resurrection bodies are like planting seeds. The grown plant comes from the seed but does not look like the seed. So our planted (buried) bodies will be raised to be something new (1 Corinthians 15:35-38). Different animals have different flesh, so our resurrected bodies will be different (1 Corinthians 15:39). Heavenly bodies—sun, moon, and stars—are different. So will we be (1 Corinthians 15:40-41).

> **It is the same way with the resurrection of the dead. Our earthly bodies are planted in the ground when we die, but they will be raised to live forever. Our bodies are buried in brokenness, but they will be raised in glory. They are buried in weakness, but they will be raised in strength. They are buried as natural human bodies, but they will be raised as spiritual bodies. For just as there are natural bodies, there are also spiritual bodies.**
> *1 Corinthians 15:42-44*

Does that clear things up? Can we now understand what resurrection life is like? No. Paul is describing as best he can what cannot be described. Imagine that you could talk to an infant in its mother's womb and that child could understand your words. All that child has known is life in the womb—dark, warm, and comfortable. How could you describe the world that child is about to enter at birth? How could you explain colors and smells and trees and flowers? When the child is born, it will leave the comfort of the world it has known and be thrust into a world of light and sound. No wonder newborns cry! But the world it enters will be more wondrous than they could have ever imagined.

So also with the resurrection world of the new heaven and earth. If this life has been full of pain and loss, then how marvelous that new life will be, but even if this life has been good in almost every way, the new life will be so much better.

Victory!

The conclusion of Paul's argument in 1 Corinthians 15 is that resurrection means victory. Victory over injustice, oppression, and agony. Victory over success, comfort, and prosperity. Victory even over death. Even victory over our fear of death.

> **Because God's children are human beings—made of flesh and blood—the Son also became flesh and blood. For only as a human being could he die, and only by dying could he break the power of the devil, who had the power of death. Only in this way could he set free all who have lived their lives as slaves to the fear of dying.** *Hebrews 2:14-15*

So we have no fear in death, because we trust ourselves to the One who defeated death once and for all. No sting in death. Death is not the end, but a glorious beginning.

For Reflection

1. Do you sometimes fear death? Why or why not?

2. Why might we find it easier to believe in the resurrection of Jesus than in our own resurrection?

3. Does prosperity make us more or less afraid of death? Why?

Living the Messiah

1. Take a few minutes each day to imagine what resurrection life will be like.

2. Give up some of your comfort for the sake of others. Find your comfort in assurance of the life to come.

Prayer

Resurrected Jesus, take away our fear of death. Give us confidence in the victory we have over death through you, our Lord and Savior.

DAY THIRTY:
WHO?

If God be for us, who can be against us?
Who shall lay anything to the charge of God's elect? It is
God that justifieth. Who is he that condemneth? It is
Christ that died, yea rather, that is risen again. Who is at
the right hand of God, Who makes intercession for us.
Romans 8:31, 33–34

When I was five years old, I went to school. I liked it so much I stayed for a few decades as a student and teacher. My life has been mainly about books and ideas. "What?" "How?" "Why?" Those were the questions I asked.

As I've gotten older, I realize more and more that the most important question in life is "Who?" That means the relationships we have with others are more significant than any idea or theory.

So Paul in Romans 8 asks a series of "who" questions to show us the certainty of God's love.

Who's Against Us?

It looks like Christians have more opposition than before. In the United States there was a time when calling yourself a Christian brought you immediate respect. My grandfather was a preacher. Everyone in his small town gave him a discount at their stores just because he was a preacher, even if they attended another church or no church at all.

Those days are gone. Today being a Christian automatically makes you suspect. Many think us hypocrites and charlatans, ready to cheat people out of their money by offering false hope. Or (what is worse) they think we use our power to abuse the innocent. I don't want to overstate the case. American Christians do not suffer persecution like those in other parts of our world. We have simply lost the privileged position we once enjoyed. The opposition does seem to grow more pronounced every year.

"Who can be against us?' It's a particularly odd question for Paul to ask. Everyone was against Paul!

> **Are they servants of Christ? I know I sound like a madman, but I have served him far more! I have worked harder, been put in prison more often, been whipped times without number, and faced death again and again. Five different times the Jewish leaders gave me thirty-nine lashes. Three times I was beaten with rods. Once I was stoned. Three times I was shipwrecked. Once I spent a whole night and a day adrift at sea. I have traveled on many long journeys. I have faced danger from rivers and from robbers. I have faced danger from my own people, the Jews, as well as from the Gentiles. I have faced danger in the cities, in the deserts, and on the seas. And I have faced danger from men who claim to be believers but are not. I have worked hard and long, enduring many sleepless nights. I have been hungry and thirsty and have often gone without food. I have shivered in the cold, without enough clothing to keep me warm.**
> *2 Corinthians 11:23-27*

Who can be against us? The more important question is "Who is for us?" God is for us. No opposition can stand against the power of the love of God. In light of that love, all resistance is futile.

Who Accuses Us?

The Bible describes Satan in many ways. Sometimes it calls him the Accuser (Job 1:6, Zechariah 3:1-2). The devil spends his time looking closely at our lives to find fault with us. And there is much fault to find. Who can stand such scrutiny? How can we defend ourselves against the charges that Satan brings against us?

We can't. But there is One who can defend us and defeat the Accuser.

> **Then I heard a loud voice shouting across the heavens:**
> **"It has come at last—**
> **salvation and power**
> **and the Kingdom of our God,**
> **and the authority of his Christ.**
> **For the accuser of our brothers and sisters**
> **has been thrown down to earth—**
> **the one who accuses them**
> **before our God day and night.**
> **And they have defeated him**
> **by the blood of the Lamb**
> **and by their testimony."** *Revelation 12:10-11*

Messiah, the Lamb, has overthrown the Accuser. The blood of Jesus removes all charges against us.

Yet some may still think that Jesus accuses us. Don't we offend Him every day by our behavior? But Paul says Jesus does not accuse. Instead He died to take away our condemnation. We sometimes forget the words that follow the most famous passage from the Bible.

For God did not send his Son into the world to condemn the world, but to save the world through him. *John 3:17 (NIV)*

Who can bring charges against us? Who can condemn us? No one. Not even ourselves.

Even if we feel guilty, God is greater than our feelings, and he knows everything. *1 John 3:20*

Who Intercedes for Us?

God is for us. No one can oppose us. Jesus died for us. No one can condemn us.

Our relationship with the Messiah is a daily walk. We rely not only on what He has done for us, but what He continues to do. He constantly defends us, pleading our case. He is always for us.

My dear children, I am writing this to you so that you will not sin. But if anyone does sin, we have an advocate who pleads our case before the Father. He is Jesus Christ, the one who is truly righteous. *1 John 2:1*

Therefore he is able, once, and forever, to save those who come to God through him. He lives forever to intercede with God on their behalf. *Hebrews 7:25*

We speak of people who "live for the weekend" or "live to go fishing" or "live for their children." Jesus lives to intercede for us. It's what He wants to do more than anything. How assuring to know that the Messiah is always on our side!

And I am convinced that nothing can ever separate us from God's love. Neither death nor life, neither angels nor demons, neither our fears for today nor our worries about tomorrow—not even the powers of hell can

separate us from God's love. No power in the sky above or in the earth below—indeed, nothing in all creation will ever be able to separate us from the love of God that is revealed in Christ Jesus our Lord. *Romans 8:38-39*

For Reflection

1. Who has been against you lately because you act like a Christian?

2. Who brings the most accusations against you?

3. Who defends us against opposition and accusation? How does He?

Living the Messiah

1. When you find yourself feeling guilty and accusing yourself of sin, think of the Messiah who forgives and defends you. He is greater than an accuser.

2. As you pray, imagine Jesus taking your case to the Father.

Prayer

Jesus, you died for us and you live for us. May we constantly make you the 'Who' in our lives. May we live in the confidence of your love.

DAY THIRTY-ONE:
WORTHY

Worthy is the Lamb that was slain, and hath redeemed us to God by His blood, to receive power, and riches, and wisdom, and strength, and honor, and glory, and blessing. Blessing and honor, glory and power, be unto Him that sitteth upon the throne, and unto the Lamb, for ever and ever.
Amen. *Revelation 5:12–14*

How much are you worth?

Financial planners speak of "net worth." It's easy to figure. You subtract your debts from your assets, and you have your bottom line, your net worth.

Surely we are worth more than that.

Or you could add up the value of the elements in your body. That comes to $1 to $5.

The government has the value of statistical life (VSL). The Department of Health and Human Services' current estimate of the value per statistical life is $13.1 million. Now that sounds more like it!

But we know we cannot put a dollar value on the life of someone we love, much less our own life.

Worth of a Dead Lamb

I don't know how much a lamb is worth. A dead lamb would be worth even less. A slaughtered lamb is not worth much at all.

Yet that is the favorite picture that the Book of Revelation uses for Jesus. Earlier in *Messiah*, we saw Jesus as "the Lamb of God that taketh away the sin of the world" (John 1:29). In Revelation, that slain Lamb, once dead but now alive, is more powerful than the most dreaded dragon (Revelation 12:11). The once dead Lamb is now a fierce Lion victorious over all His enemies (Revelation 5:5).

What is that Lamb, the Messiah, worth?

As we have worked our way through the words of *Messiah,* we experience the entire story of Jesus. John the Baptist cries out in the wilderness, calling for a highway for the one who is to come. The Lord God shakes heaven and earth to bring in the Desire of all Nations who will purify His people. To us a child is born. Shepherds come and worship Him. He is the Great Shepherd who feeds His flock and gives them rest.

Then He is despised and rejected. He bears our sins and sorrows. He is the Lamb that is rejected, yet who bears the sins of the world. He is cut off from the land of the living.

God does not leave His soul in hell. The Lord gives the word and the proclamation comes. He is the King of Kings and Lords of Lords! He lives! Risen from the grave! And he is the New Adam who brings resurrection life to all humanity. He lives forever to intercede for us.

What is this Messiah worth?

As *Messiah* says, "Power, and riches, and wisdom, and strength, and honor, and glory, and blessing."

He deserves all power. "I have been given all authority in heaven and on earth" (Matthew 28:18). All that exists belongs to him. He is the source of all wisdom and knowledge. Nothing can stand against His strength. All honor is due Him as King of Kings. He reigns in glory. All things bless and praise Him.

Jesus, the Messiah, the Lamb, is worthy of power, and riches, and wisdom, and strength, and honor, and glory, and blessing. We could multiply the words and they still would not fully describe His worth.

Worth of the One Who Reigns

We sing in *Messiah,* "Blessing and honor, glory and power, be unto Him that sitteth upon the throne."

How much is God worth?

We use the word "God" so much that we lose sight of how breath-takingly astounding God is. Find a dark place and look at the night sky. Try to look beyond the farthest star. God is there. He is somehow larger than the universe. At the same time, it staggers us to think that He knows each of us intimately. He is so big that He can care for the smallest desire of each of the eight billion people on earth. He commands countless angels, yet He knows when even a single sparrow falls to the ground (Matthew 10:29).

When we praise God as the Almighty, we are only recognizing a tiny bit of His worth.

> **Remember the things I have done in the past.**
> **For I alone am God!**
> **I am God, and there is none like me.**
> **Only I can tell you the future before it even happens.**
> **Everything I plan will come to pass, for I do whatever I**
> **wish.** *Isaiah 46:9-10*

> Oh, how great are God's riches and wisdom and knowledge! How impossible it is for us to understand his decisions and his ways!
> For who can know the Lord's thoughts?
> Who knows enough to give him advice?
> And who has given him so much
> that he needs to pay it back?
> For everything comes from him and exists by his power and is intended for his glory. All glory to him forever! Amen. *Romans 11:33-36*

How to Recognize Worth

How can we recognize the worth of God and the Lamb? How do we respond to the Messiah?

The same way as those in Revelation respond. The same way *Messiah* is a response.

We sing!

And we join countless others who sing of the glory of God and the Lamb.

> Then I looked again, and I heard the voices of thousands and millions of angels around the throne and of the living beings and the elders. And they sang in a mighty chorus:
> "Worthy is the Lamb who was slaughtered— to receive power and riches and wisdom and strength and honor and glory and blessing."
> And then I heard every creature in heaven and on earth and under the earth and in the sea. They sang:
> "Blessing and honor and glory and power belong to the one sitting on the throne and to the Lamb forever and ever."

And the four living beings said, "Amen!" And the twenty-four elders fell down and worshiped the Lamb. *Revelation 24:11-14*

We sing with millions of angels. We sing with all the faithful people who have gone to be with the Lord. We sing with every creature on earth and in the heavens. We sing because there is no other way to give glory to the Messiah. We sing with our voices. We sing with our lives. Glory to God and to the Lamb! This is the playlist, the theme song, of our very being. Amen.

For Reflection

1. How much is Jesus worth to you?

2. How much is God worth to you?

3. What are some ways we express their worthiness?

Living the Messiah

1. Sing along with a recording of *Messiah.*

2. Write your own song, at least your own words, that give praise to God and the Messiah.

Prayer

Lord God, Messiah, open our hearts to bask in your worth. Open our lips to praise you in song.

ABOUT
KHARIS PUBLISHING:

Kharis Publishing, an imprint of Kharis Media LLC, is a leading Christian and inspirational book publisher based in Aurora, Chicago metropolitan area, Illinois. Kharis' dual mission is to give voice to under-represented writers (including women and first-time authors) and equip orphans in developing countries with literacy tools. That is why, for each book sold, the publisher channels some of the proceeds into providing books and computers for orphanages in developing countries so that these kids may learn to read, dream, and grow. For a limited time, Kharis Publishing is accepting unsolicited queries for nonfiction (Christian, self-help, memoirs, business, health and wellness) from qualified leaders, professionals, pastors, and ministers. Learn more at: https://kharispublishing.com/

www.ingramcontent.com/pod-product-compliance
Lightning Source LLC
Chambersburg PA
CBHW051424090426
42737CB00014B/2820